P9-CDS-928

Beyond Consequences, Logic, and Control

A Love Based Approach to Helping Children With Severe Behaviors

ALSO BY HEATHER FORBES

Beyond Consequences, Logic and Control, Volume 1,
Spanish Edition

Beyond Consequences, Logic and Control, Volume 1,
Russian Edition

Beyond Consequences, Logic and Control, Volume 2

Dare to Love: The Art of Merging Science and Love
into Parenting Children with Difficult Behaviors

100 Daily Parenting Reflections

www.beyondconsequences.com

Beyond Consequences, Logic, and Control

A Love Based Approach to Helping Children With Severe Behaviors

Heather T. Forbes, LCSW

B. Bryan Post

Beyond Consequences Institute

Beyond Consequences, Logic, and Control

A Love Based
Approach to
Helping Children
With Severe Behaviors

Copyright © 2009 Heather T. Forbes
Registration Number TX 7-080-025

Library of Congress Control Number: 2005938436
ISBN 0-9777040-0-9, 978-0-9777040-0-2

Second Edition 2010

Published by:
Beyond Consequences Institute, LLC
Boulder, CO

Dedication

∎

This book is dedicated to my children, Ben and Joanna. The life lessons you taught me far outweigh any that I could ever teach you as a mother. Thank you, also, for putting me on my own healing journey and helping me know that love never fails.

–Heather T. Forbes

This work is dedicated to my wife, Kristi, and our two beautiful daughters, Mikalah and Marley. Thank you for teaching me that love always exists. And to two of the most significant men who touched and gave my life meaning: My father, Billie R. Post 1941-2004, and my friend and mentor, Lawrence G. Anderson 1937-2004.

–B. Bryan Post

Check out the
Beyond Consequences Institute
website today to:

- Sign-up on our network and receive announcements of future free events such as teleseminars and lectures.

- Receive Heather's free eNewsletter for more Q&A support.

- Download free articles that will further your understanding of the Beyond Consequences Model.

- Learn how you can have Heather T. Forbes, LCSW in your area to hold a seminar or workshop.

- Purchase additional copies of this book for teachers, friends, and family members.

- View videos of how this model works when parents make the commitment to move from fear to love.

www.beyondconsequences.com

Table of Contents

■

Foreword

∎

Heather T. Forbes and B. Bryan Post address some of the most pressing and challenging issues faced by parents of children with histories of disrupted attachments.

The authors have the ability to strip away the fog surrounding these troubled relationships, exposing the reality of children's reactions and dysregulated responses to the past traumatic experiences that so often underlie their difficulty in making close, affectional bonds.

This clarity illuminates their therapeutic intervention in a manner that allows parent and child to hold on to the strategy, as they are caught up in the whirlwind of challenging behavior during the painful process of change.

The authors address in detail the child's trauma (often associated with the adoption process), and they also address the painful struggle of the parents when a challenging child exposes the parents' own vulnerabilities to memories that they may have suppressed of their own past experiences.

The immense value of this book is the clarity and simplicity of the authors' working model; the price of this clarity is that the hard truth is exposed with such intensity that some may shy away from facing reality and not benefit from their undoubted insights.

The psychotherapeutic intervention described by the authors involves clinicians tapping into their own empathic capacities to help children feel supported to such a degree that a direct connection can be forged between the reality of children's traumatic experiences and the parents and/or clinicians being able to tolerate their pain, and so regulate the child's distress down to a manageable level. The recognition that another person can truly understand and tolerate their pain can be a major contribution to the client's therapeutic outcome.

This book is an absolute necessity for every parent working through attachment issues, and for every professional (therapist, caseworker, teacher, policy maker, etc.) working with children who exhibit severe acting-out behaviors.

–Sir Richard Bowlby, Attachment Advocate

A Note to the Reader
■

"The longest journey is the journey inward."
– Dag Hammarskjold, Swedish Diplomat

There is a stream of sorrow that continues to flow through my heart. It is flowing from the past pain of parenting my own children out of a place of control and fear instead of a place of love and compassion. I started my parenting journey ten years ago on a plane to Russia with my husband and then one year later on another plane to Russia to adopt our daughter. After adopting our children, we realized that we were in desperate need of help. Seeking help from specialist after specialist led us to become parents who were forcing attachment and working to make our children change. Our home was constantly filled with an undercurrent of anger, resentment, and fear. I hated being a parent. I hated always trying to stay one step ahead of the defiance. I hated always having to control behavior in order to assure safety for our future. Sorrow, pain, and perpetual fear continued to pervade our every interaction. Today, this river of sorrow runs in a dark place within my heart.

After making a paradigm shift from fear to love, not only did change become a reality, but also healing began. Healing for all family members became possible. Now looking back, it amazes me, and it is painfully difficult to ponder how we as people born of love easily lose our way to fear. How did I begin from a place of love to only find myself literally trembling in fear and sorrow?

Fear has the ability to constrict us in seeing only the negative, and it distorts our ability to think clearly and rationally. In this state of fear, I diligently read and read and reread every book I could find. I read every journal article, joined every Internet list serve, and hunted down professionals in the field of attachment in order to find answers. I easily bought into the methods presented to me by the professionals. I found myself highlighting in bright yellow and circling in thick red ink every explanation that my children were intentionally manipulating me, that my children were devising plans to successfully triangulate me and my husband, and that my children were unable to receive or give love. My frantic search only confirmed my fears of my children growing up to be criminals or adults diagnosed with mental disorders such as anti-social personality disorder or borderline personality disorder. My fears soon became my reality for parenting.

As I look back now and as I sit down to write my part of this book, I feel my entire body ignite. Every time I begin a new chapter, every time I reread a chapter for editing, every time I look through the books on my desk written to explain what creates attachment, my arms literally become weak, my stomach twists into a series of knots, and 1,000 pins prickle in my back. Beyond that, I feel my soul weeping because it is not about parenting from a place of control. It is not about parenting "disturbed" or "hurt" or "unattached" children. It is not about stopping at every moment to "make" attachment happen.

Parenting a child with a traumatic history is about learning to interpret the child's reactions to past experiences from a place of compassion, understanding, and love. Love really is enough when it is given in the absence of fear. It takes seeing your child for who he is and meeting your child in his pain. It is not just meeting your child in his behavior or even at the surface of his feelings, but truly meeting your child in the depths of his fear—in the depths of his soul. It is about meeting your child in a place of complete and utter darkness where pain beyond human tolerance resides.

It takes courage and it takes being willing to feel your own pain first and then to take on the pain of your child. Fear is ever present in our lives, especially in every interaction with our children with severe behaviors. Fear has to be acknowledged and fear has to be brought to a conscious level. We have to stop being fearful of the fear and we need to find the courage to move through the fear in order to bring the light of love into the darkness of our children's wounds. We have to stop feeding more fear into our families through the traditional approaches and we have to be willing to trust that our children still are creatures of love, despite their past experiences of fear.

I invite you to read the following chapters with an open heart and an open mind. I invite you to see the fear in the traditional model of working with children and to see that parents do not have to give up their need to give love to their children. I offer you a more loving, compassionate, and truthful explanation of behaviors.

Thank you for joining me in this book; I pray it restores hope and gives you reassurance for what you have probably known all along...*love never fails* (1 Corinthians 13:8).

–Heather T. Forbes, LCSW

A Second Note to the Reader

This book will be controversial because it dispels old beliefs and seeks to replace them with new ideas. In our humble opinion, the attachment therapy literature is fraught with harsh, threatening and fear-laden approaches to dealing with children. These approaches over time lead to increasingly resentful parents who feel hopeless and helpless to deal with their children's increasingly challenging behaviors. Many of the techniques provided to parents by well-meaning professionals have led to disrupted placements, medication increases, residential placements, and ultimately, broken hearts. It is difficult to be non-judgmental when it comes to the pain of children and parents, yet we have done our best to offer a clear presentation for the reader to compare and contrast the common beliefs and approaches about these children and their behaviors.

After years of working with families who have struggled time and again with severe behaviors such as lying, stealing, and hoarding, we want to offer our insights to help both parents and professionals deal with such behaviors more effectively and successfully.

As is well known, the behaviors we will be discussing are commonly linked to the psychiatric diagnosis of reactive attachment disorder (RAD). Though we are theoretically opposed to the labeling of children for myriad reasons, reactive attachment disorder is the buzz diagnosis for the moment with which most are familiar. In this regard, we have taken some of the most severe behaviors associated with children in this category and offer both parents and professionals insights into these behaviors that are contrary to popular opinion. It is typically espoused in the field of attachment therapy that traditional therapy approaches are not effective in treating children with reactive attachment disorder. We would like to take that a step further by stating that "Traditional *attachment* therapy approaches are not effective in treating children with reactive attachment disorder." We are referring to the behaviors that are addressed in each chapter, but also to the treatment of "reactive attachment disorder" itself.

When one hears about treatment, then it naturally implies applying a methodical approach geared towards eliminating symptoms. However, there is more to treatment than merely the elimination of symptoms. Offering cough syrup to a child with a cold is sufficient for eliminating symptoms, but if measures are not taken to also support and enhance the child's immune system through encouraging rest, extra vitamin C, and nurturing (which assist in supporting the stress response system), then the cold may eventually turn into pneumonia. Rather than just addressing symptoms for behavioral change, efforts must be directed towards the healing of the underlying causes, thus bringing about behavioral change.

The following pages will challenge what you have traditionally heard or read in the past about children and severe behaviors. By utilizing a sound and prudent theoretical approach along with a common sense understanding, both rooted in solid research and empirically tested techniques, we will provide a new perspective for understanding severe behaviors and will offer you step-by-step analysis for how to deal with these behaviors with your own children.

We have taken this a step further by conducting an intensive meta-analysis of the most common approaches and views of these severe behaviors from a traditional perspective, taking the time and effort to document carefully each view, then providing both a "traditional" and a "new" perspective of each behavior. We have done this to ensure that we are not being biased – preferring our approach to another – but rather are giving you, the reader, a clear understanding of why we look at things the way we do and why we make the corresponding recommendations.

–B. Bryan Post

PART ONE

The Principles of a New Understanding

CHAPTER ONE

The Stress Model
■

"Action without understanding only leads you back to darkness."
– B. Bryan Post

In each section to follow, you will find a definition of the problem behavior and then a perspective on each behavior from what we call the "Traditional View" and "A New View." As you read the new view perspective, it is important to keep in mind four key principles that create the foundation for the understanding and techniques being offered. The full understanding of the four principles will enable you to understand and be aligned with chapters that follow. It is our goal that these four principles empower you as a parent to feel equipped to apply the understanding and techniques to help your child with any behavior he presents to you.

Our belief is that many of the things we do are based on and driven by our understanding. The things we do are not done to be mean or intentionally cruel, but are done from the perception and understanding within us. Our actions are directed, guided, and aligned with the core principles within our understanding. Everything we do can ultimately be traced back to the guiding principles from which we operate. Thus, it is imperative that you read and reread this section as often as possible to fully comprehend the new perspective.

So read, and then reread this chapter on the Stress Model before you attempt to fully delve into your understanding of the behaviors – before reading the following seven chapters.

A New View
Four Key Principles

1. All negative behavior arises from an unconscious, fear-based state of stress.

2. There are only two primary emotions: **Love** and **Fear.**

3. There is both **negative** and **positive repetitious conditioning.** We are all conditioned to behave in various ways, both good and bad.

> 4. **Negative and positive neurophysiologic feedback loops**
> exist beyond our conscious awareness. They occur at an uncon-
> scious, physiologic level, and we have the ability to change or add
> to these feedback loops.

The New View that will be discussed in this book is based on four key
principles. First, all negative behavior arises from an unconscious, fear-
based state of stress. Second, there are only two primary emotions, love
and fear. Third, there is both negative and positive repetitious conditioning.
We are all conditioned to behave in various ways, both good and bad. And
fourth, negative and positive neurophysiologic feedback loops exist beyond
our conscious awareness. They occur at an unconscious physiologic level
and we have the ability to change or add to these feedback loops. Let's take
each principle and break it down.

PRINCIPLE #1
All negative behavior arises from an unconscious,
fear-based state of stress.

It was once said to me, "Scared children do scary things." The simple
truth in this wise statement is that while we believe that children are perfectly
capable of making clear and rational decisions, we also need to believe the
opposite – that children are incapable of making clear and rational decisions.
In fact, stress research helps us to understand just that. In times of stress,
our thinking processes become confused and distorted.[1] Not only are we not
thinking clearly when stressed, but the very framework of our understanding is challenged in that moment by what we can believe and remember. For
not only does our thinking become confused and distorted, our short-term
memory system becomes suppressed. This means that when children act out
in a disturbing manner, they are not only confused and overwhelmed, but
they cannot even remember what is safe and what is not safe.

Traditionally, we have seen children as being willfully disobedient and
manipulative. This stems from a belief that in the moments of being disobedient and manipulative, they also have full cognitive and conscious awareness of their actions. Unfortunately for both parents and children, this could
not be further from the truth. Stress constricts their thinking, distorts their
perspective, and short-circuits their short-term memory.

Children diagnosed with reactive attachment disorder, oppositional-defiant disorder, bipolar, and other such psychiatric diagnoses, have almost all experienced some degree of trauma in their lifetimes. The trauma can be anywhere on the continuum – from mild, to moderate, to severe. Generally the children we will be referring to in the following pages have experienced specific traumas along the moderate to severe range. And what is significant is that for most of these children, the earliest traumas experienced have since been compounded and overlaid with more childhood trauma. Examples of such trauma can be seen in the following chart.

Examples of Childhood Traumas	
• Physical Abuse	• Automobile Accident
• Sexual Abuse	• Pre and Perinatal Birth Trauma
• Emotional Abuse	• Loss of Caregiver
• Neglect	• Depressed Parental Care
• Adoption	• Prolonged Experiences of Unmet Needs
• Foster Care	• Bullying
• Surrogacy	• Domestic Violence
• Frequent Moves	• Medical Trauma

Childhood traumas are not limited to those on this list.

When a child experiences trauma, the child's ability to develop a sufficient regulatory system is severely compromised. In cases of severe trauma, the child's life is literally at risk. For these children, their internal survival mechanisms then become activated, dedicating all the body's resources to remain alert in "survival mode." These children perceive the world as threatening from a neurological, physical, emotional, cognitive, and social perspective. They operate from a paradigm of fear to ensure their safety and security. Hence, what is seen is an overly stressed-out child who has difficulty interacting in relationships, who struggles to behave in a loving way, who quite often cannot think clearly, and who swings back and forth in his emotional states due to an underdeveloped regulatory system. While perceived by most professionals as dangerous, a child of trauma is essentially a scared child – a stressed child living out of a primal, survival mode in order to maintain his existence.

These traumatic experiences are stored, and for most children are buried, as unprocessed and unexpressed memories within the body/mind system. According to neuroscientist Bruce D. Perry, M.D., we have four levels of memory: cognitive, emotional, motor, and state.[2] It is in the deepest level of memory, the state memory, that these experiences are stored. The significance of this is that when our state memory is activated, it directs all of our responses. It has the ability to dominate over the other three memory states. To understand this further, let us take a look at all four of our memory states: cognitive, emotional, motor, and state.

Cognitive. Our cognitive memory allows us to have immediate recall. It is the level of memory where we store facts, data, dates, research, names, numbers, etc. We generally have immediate access to this level of memory.

Emotional. For every cognitive memory, there is a corresponding emotional memory attached to it. However, at the emotional level, the cognitive and emotional memories may not always be easily connected. You may not always have access to the cognitive memory, even though you may have access to the emotional memory. For example, say you have a friend from high school or college that you have not seen for some years. While you can remember the face, you are unable to remember the name. Yet, attached to the memory of the face of this person is a very pleasant and warm feeling – the emotional memory. Additionally, events happening in our lives which are emotionally impacting become easily accessible at the emotional level of memory. If you were asked where you were on 9/11, you would probably remember the exact time of day and your location when you received the news of the terrorist attacks. However, if I asked you where you were last Friday, your memory of this day would more than likely be clouded, at best. This memory is not easily accessible because the events that happened on that day were probably not emotionally significant.

Motor. The motor memory is our body level of memory. For the most part, we seldom think about this level of memory and operate on automatic pilot. When you get into your car and begin driving, you seldom think about pulling open the door handle, putting the key into the ignition, or putting your arm over the passenger seat as you begin to back up. As you continue in the automatic mode, you have suddenly arrived at work and think, "How did I get here?" This level of memory is very unconscious.

State. The state level of memory is the level of memory most associated with your personality traits. It lies in direct reference point to your brainstem. In other words, it is located in your lower limbic system or your reptilian brain. This area of your brain is not part of your rational brain but rather a part of your emotional brain. It is responsible for processing raw data from the environment and sending immediate signals of fight, flee, or freeze. This holds great significance for traumatized children due to the fact that traumatic memories get stored at the state level. When a person reaches a heightened state of stress, this state memory gets triggered, thereby releasing all previous relevant memories into the upper memory banks. In this manner, when a child with a traumatic history is confronted with a situation which heightens his level of stress, the child's state memory becomes activated. Rapid-fire communications to the other areas of the memory system are initiated, informing the child that the current situation is threatening. Additionally, this rapid-fire communication is also telling the child that this situation is almost guaranteed to workout like a previously stored experience. In other words, in the midst of a stressful or perceived threatening event, this child, due to his cognitively distorted state of mind, is likely to believe deep within the very cells of his body that if he doesn't convince this person right now that he is telling the truth, then in all likelihood he might be abused, abandoned, neglected, or worse – he might die! Faced with this looming threat, this child is most likely going to tell a lie, despite his understanding at the cognitive level that lies are morally and ethically wrong. In the midst of stress and threat, the state memory can completely override all other memory states.

Now it may seem like a far stretch to consider such possibilities for this child, especially over something as simple as stealing a cookie. You're asking, "How can stealing a cookie be linked to the threat of death?" Yet, nothing could come closer to truly understanding this child's experience when confronted with the theft of a cookie. His state level of memory is activated, linking past traumatic experiences to the present situation. Thus, it is no longer just about the cookie. For the child, it is about survival – life or death. Through the comprehension of this fear dynamic, we can begin to understand why such children are prone to repetitive, negative behaviors, such as lying. If you had the belief at the cellular level that lying would ensure your survival and safety, wouldn't you continue this behavior?

All the behaviors discussed in this book are based on one simple model: The Stress Model. The Stress Model was developed by this author, Bryan Post, as a model to explain human behavior. The Stress Model is a regulatory theory of human behavior based on findings from the field of neurophysiology and studies regarding affect regulation. It really is simple, so read on....

According to the Stress Model, all behavior arises from a state of stress; and between the behavior and the stress is the presence of a primary emotion. There are only two primary emotions: Love and Fear. It is through the expression, processing, and understanding of the primary emotion that you can calm the stress and diminish the behavior.

When the stress model is understood, it can be applied to any complex family situation in order to find a simple, loving approach to help all family members. We must first see that there are only two emotions: *love and fear*. From love, only loving *feelings* – such as joy and happiness – can be present. From love, only loving *behaviors* – such as reciprocity, empathy, conscience, and the ability to understand deeply the experience of others – can be exhibited. Likewise, from fear, only fear-based *feelings* – such as anger, frustration, shame, blame, and envy – can be present. From fear, only fear-based *behaviors* – such as hitting, fighting, arguing, lying, stealing, defiance and hostility – can be exhibited (see chart below).

When seeking to understand children of trauma, we must fully comprehend that at their deepest core is an emotional state of fear. What we see on the outside is anger, defiance, stealing, killing animals, setting fires, etc. These fear-based behaviors rapidly create fear within us. Thus, we become constricted and angered by the behaviors that can literally scare us to death.

THE STRESS MODEL

Behavior arises from stress; in between stress and behavior is a primary emotion: Love or Fear.

BEHAVIOR

LOVE   EMOTION   FEAR

STRESS

Triggering Sensory Event

Remember, however, that these are merely behaviors – manifestations of the fear that is underneath it all. In order to change these scary behaviors, we must first address the fear. When we are able to help our child calm his fear, the fear-based behaviors will dissipate. As you read through the following chapters, examples will be given to show how simple parenting responses can accomplish this. The hardest part of implementing this model will be in dealing with your own fear that arises from the behaviors of your child. This is a critical part of your parenting because in order to help your child move out of his fear, you must have first addressed your own fear. Impossible? No. Difficult? Yes.

What makes this difficult is that neither children nor adults are fully conscious of their initial states of stress that occur at the body level. Before we ever become aware of it consciously or cognitively, we will have already had a stress reaction. For simplicity's sake, but not to downplay the profound impact of this dynamic, let us take the example of hearing a door slam. Immediately upon hearing the slam, you have a startle reaction; your body becomes suddenly alert. Before you will have had any conscious or cognitive awareness of exactly what made you startle, your body will have already reacted. This is considered to be an unconscious reaction. Candace Pert, the author of the ground-breaking book, *Molecules of Emotion*, tells us that any visual cue – or anything that we see with our eyes – must pass through seven different synapses in our brain before it ever becomes an actual conscious thought.[3]

The implications for this, as it applies to children who are overly sensitive due to traumatic experience (you do not have a child diagnosed Reactive Attachment Disorder or Oppositional Defiant Disorder without some degree of trauma in his history) are profound. The majority of early development and interaction for a child is emotionally driven; hence, the majority of childhood engagement is unconscious. Considering this, we must understand that when a child feels stressed or threatened to any degree, his behavior will arise from an unconscious place. There is no such thing as willful disobedience or manipulation without first the seeds of fear and stress.

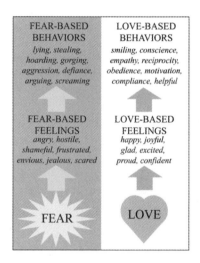

FEAR-BASED BEHAVIORS	LOVE-BASED BEHAVIORS
lying, stealing, hoarding, gorging, aggression, defiance, arguing, screaming	*smiling, conscience, empathy, reciprocity, obedience, motivation, compliance, helpful*

FEAR-BASED FEELINGS	LOVE-BASED FEELINGS
angry, hostile, shameful, frustrated, envious, jealous, scared	*happy, joyful, glad, excited, proud, confident*

| FEAR | LOVE |

Remember that the negative behaviors we will be discussing have arisen first from an unconscious, fear-based place of stress, as opposed to any clear cognitive or conscious place. Stress causes confused and distorted thinking: therefore, if a child has done or is doing something that you know is not in line with a loving relationship, the child must obviously be coming from a place of stress and fear. And certainly if the child had the conscious ability to recognize such a state, he would begin making attempts to do so; however, with such behavior being unconscious, in that moment the child is doing the best that he can to survive.

CHAPTER TWO

Love and Fear

∎

"There is no fear in love. But perfect love drives out fear."
– 1 John 4:18

PRINCIPLE #2
There are only two primary emotions: Love and Fear.

In our society, we have a tendency to view anger as a primary emotion. In fact, when we consider children to be willfully disobedient, manipulative, or controlling, we perceive this as stemming from an internal place of anger. The traditional attachment perspective is based entirely on the perception that, following a period of unmet needs, a child becomes filled with rage and mistrust of the world. The following description is echoed in virtually every reactive attachment disorder text, parenting book, or article that has been written during the last twenty years.

> *If there is a severe shortage or lack of reciprocal interactions, babies experience a tremendous amount of rage, believe that those who are supposed to love them and care for them will only hurt them, and come to view the world as an extremely hostile environment in which no one can be trusted. Babies who have the misfortune to have such dire experiences fail to form a secure sense of attachment to anyone. We refer to these babies as attachment disordered. Without extensive, appropriate psychotherapy and parenting (because they don't view others as having any importance), children with attachment disorder are doomed to a life of hurting others.[1]*

The above statement is such a common belief that it is not even questioned by most professionals in the field of attachment therapy. We have come to view these children as fundamentally rageful children who are out to control the world and everyone in it. Such distorted views on children's inner worlds following neglect or abuse arise straight out of the works of Foster Cline, M.D., the co-founder of the Cline-Fay Institute in Golden, Colorado, and seen by many as the father of modern day attachment therapy. Cline adapted a therapeutic approach used to treat infantile autism, called Rage Reduction therapy[2], into his work with children in residential care, again, based on the misconception that following prolonged periods of hurt or neglect children become filled with rage. If one were to really analyze the current popular methods being used by attachment professionals and instructed to parents today, we could clearly establish that, although professionals no longer conduct therapy sessions as Cline did during the 70's and 80's, most of the consequence-based parenting approaches are still geared towards "breaking" a child's will and "teaching" children that they must trust adults.

Considering the science of the day during the 70's, one might be forgiving of Cline for his conceptualizations regarding abused children; however, in spite of all of the research we now have available to us and a much deeper and profound understanding of the brain, Cline continues to be a proponent of his consequence-based parenting approaches which see traumatized children as fundamentally angry and controlling. Therefore, he has done little to influence the current-day hoards of practitioners who continue to follow the foundation he established years ago.

Even Doctor Spock apologized years later for his role in encouraging parents to let their babies cry themselves to sleep! In the end, Spock believed such practices were ultimately traumatic to young babies. It takes quite an individual to come back years later and right a wrong publicly.

What has previously been labeled in children as anger-based control, manipulation, defiance, and even the hurting of one's self or the killing of animals, is not based in anger, but based in fear. This principle may be very difficult to grasp initially because we live in a fear-based society and anger is generally our immediate reaction to a threatening event. Seldom do we actually experience ourselves as being afraid. This emotion of fear, however, is the root of our anger. We avoid it because it feels safer to be in a place of anger (a protective feeling), while we feel exposed and vulnerable to be in a place of fear.

A developmental pediatrician with a generalist knowledge of the brain will tell you that when a child cries, he is experiencing a state of stress and fear. A cry is a universal signal of distress. According to traditional views on attachment, when a caregiver does not interrupt an infant's cry, the infant becomes mistrusting and full of rage. This belief is both misleading and incorrect. Rather than becoming rageful and mistrusting, the infant becomes overwhelmingly stressed out and afraid. If this state continues for prolonged, indefinite periods of time, what subsequently results is a child ill-equipped to sooth his own elevated states of stress. And we then have a child who is unable to contend with the world, a child prone to overstimulation. What we eventually see is a SCARED child, NOT a RAGEFUL child. This understanding makes all of the difference. Candace Pert, in her book, *Molecules of Emotion*, gives an account of her realization of the understanding of fear after hearing these words spoken to her: "If you look underneath your depression, you'll find anger. Look under your anger, and you'll find sadness. And under sadness is the root of it all, what's really masquerading all the while – fear."[3]

To comprehend this fully, we must look closely at the definition of fear: **fear is an internal stress reaction to a perceived threat that lies internal to the body-mind or external to the body-mind.** Any external or internal stimulus perceived by the body-mind system as a threat can cause a fear reaction. Some accepted and common stimuli include being afraid of the dark, the boogeyman, or death. Yet, more common, but more often overlooked examples include parental pressure, television, group activities, mealtime, bedtime, transition periods (moving from one place to the next can be considered a transition), and even brushing teeth or doing chores. All of these activities, plus many more, are very often the events that cause children to experience initial levels of heightened stress and fear. We need to recognize that stress-inducing stimuli, whatever they may be, enter the body through our sensory pathways: sight, sound, touch, smell, taste, and body temperature. Any one pathway can cause the body to accelerate into stress and fear.

Let us pause at this point to recognize one very important point: **All stress is not bad.** In fact, most scientists hesitate to consider that there is even a bad state of stress. Stress is critical to life and survival. It is needed to defend against illnesses and viruses. In fact, it is an unavoidable aspect of our lives. Just to wake up is to experience a state of stress. To laugh is to experience stress. The reason many hesitate to consider it bad at all is because it is a reaction the body has that is based in survival. Even for the most stressed out individual whose stress is leading to high blood pressure and ulcers, these are signals the body is sending that something is not right and action needs to be taken in order to return to optimal functioning. Without these, we might not ever go to the physician for a check-up. Therefore, stress is not bad; it is simply not always pleasurable.

As Principle # 2 states, there are only two primary emotions: love and fear. One definition of love is the space that exists between two people. Poets for centuries have attempted to define love. The reality is that you cannot adequately define the experience of love. The moment you have defined it, it becomes something else – that which you have defined. I have found one of the best ways to consider love is to understand that love is what we bring to the space that surrounds us. Love is not possessive or controlling. It simply exists in the present space and time. Any two people are capable of experiencing love at any given moment if they are able to put aside their fears and preconceived notions for what love is supposed to be. **Love is being fully present in the moment.**

To love a child is merely to be present with her, to not be thinking about work, chores, or the day's duties, but rather to be present, attuned, and in harmony with the child's needs and desires. Not that you will give in to every need, want, or desire, but you will open yourself up with the ability to be present to her without judgment or a need to change her; this is to love a child.

Let's spend just a moment discussing the brain. A discussion on the brain is important to fully understanding the dynamics of love and fear. You might be asking, "The brain? Why is understanding the brain so important?" Bruce Perry, M.D. has stated that if you work with children and you do not have a generalist understanding of the brain, then you are missing out on a whole spectrum of childhood behavior.[4] In as much as this statement is true, simply an understanding of how the brain works is not sufficient. There are many who claim to understand the brain and comprehend much of what we are going to be discussing next. However, in the words of Stephen Covey, "To know, but not to do, is to not know." In other words, simply knowing something is not sufficient. Our comprehension of a subject must transcend merely the subject itself and be applicable throughout every day life. "Principles," as Dr. Covey states, "are universal. They do not change from situation to situation. They are as consistent as the day."[5] In other words, what goes on in your child's brain must also go on in your brain, my brain, and even your child's psychiatrist's brain. Underneath the surface we are all pretty much the same; we only vary in degrees. Research is beginning to establish that these degrees of differences have as much to do with nature as with nurture.

An important point when discussing the brain is that **one cannot separate one area of the brain from another.** When one area of the brain becomes activated, essentially the entire body-mind system becomes activated. The following summary of the amygdala, hippocampus, and orbito-frontal cortex are offered to stimulate the reader's interest in the brain by providing some very general information. The following statements are generally accepted in the scientific community. However, the brain is composed of literally millions of aspects and every single one is of great importance, so, while this discussion is simplified, it by no means is comprehensive and is not intended to minimize the importance of all the brain's systems. For our purposes of discussing stress, trauma, and social/emotional relationships, there are three areas of the brain that are of primary importance: the amygdala, the hippocampus, and the orbito-frontal cortex.

Amygdala. While we will call this part of the brain the amygdala, there are, in fact, two lobes to the amygdala, scientifically referred to as the amygdalii. This area of the brain lies at the base of the brain above the brainstem and is considered to be a part of the lower limbic system. It completes its development within the first 18 months after the child is born; however, there is evidence that this area of the brain is already online and fully active while still in utero. In this manner, it is a part of our primal, less evolved brain. It is responsible for sensing threat in the environment and initiating the start of the body-mind's fast paced stress reaction system. It can most easily be considered a part of our reactive brain. Joseph LeDoux – in his book *The Emotional Brain* – explains: "in the presence of danger of stimuli that warn of danger, behavioral, autonomic, and endocrine responses are expressed, and reflexes are modulated. Each of these responses is controlled by a different set of outputs from the central nucleus of that amygdala."[6] Thus, stress hormones in the brain originate from the amygdala.

This area of the brain is oftentimes referred to in Psychology 101 when discussing the fight or flight pattern. However, a third reaction has been added over the past twenty years and that reaction is "freeze." Scientists are now able to determine that our freeze reaction is in fact our initial reaction to a threatening event. We all go through it, some of us more rapidly than others. When you hear a loud, startling noise, your first reaction is not to hit the person next to you or jump up and start running, it's actually to freeze first and then determine your next movement. This very simple re-explanation of the fight or flight reaction can allow us to reconsider how we fundamentally view children and other adults. Rather than perceiving individuals as becoming angry first, or seeking to run away, we must now reconsider this age-old tenet of fight or flight to take into consideration the initial reaction of freeze. When the caveman saw the Saber Tooth Tiger perched upon the tree limb waiting to pounce, he did not immediately get angry or even take off running; rather, he froze and thought, "Oh my, gosh!" It was then that he ran for his life!

Hippocampus. Again, often times this part of the brain is referred to as the hippocampii in scientific circles due to the presence of two lobes. This area of the brain is primarily responsible for our ability to think clearly in the midst of stressful situations by calling upon our short-term memory. The hippocampus does not complete its development until well into the thirty-sixth month after the child has been born. Up until this point (at the age of three), children are not fully equipped to calm themselves or even relax themselves into sufficient sleep. The hippocampus is directly involved in being able to help calm the outpourings of the amygdala by sending a memory message to remind the amygdala of a similar past experience, thereby creating a correlation with the current experience. We never lose a single memory. Our memories get stored away into the filing cabinet of our mind when they are no longer needed and can then be recalled when necessary. The hippocampus sits directly in the right hemisphere, but it, along with the orbito-frontal cortex, controls the thinking, left-hemisphere of the brain. Therefore, when the amygdala perceives a threat of any nature, it sends a major signal to the hippocampus seeking some correlation with a past experience. Dependent on the past experience, the individual is then able to make a significant correlation or contrast and then move forward from there. In the case of some children, they become unable to move at all, but rather remain frozen. We will discuss this following a brief overview of the orbito-frontal cortex and regulatory system.

Orbito-frontal cortex. This area of the brain is recognized as the executive control center for all of our social and emotional functioning. The orbito-frontal cortex sits at the front of the brain and assists us in reading facial expressions, tone of voice, body language, and posture. By doing so, it supports us in effectively navigating social and emotional relationships with others. Allan Schore at the UCLA School of Medicine informs us that the frontal lobe of the cortex is the key area in both infant attachment and emotional regulation. It receives both external sensory stimulation and visceral information from the body's internal environment. It connects the facial expression of the mother with what the infant is feeling at the time. If it is intense pleasure, one set of nerve fibers is enhanced; if it is intense pain or fear, a different set is cultivated.[7] It tells us to not smile when someone else is crying and to stand still when a dog is growling at our knees. Both the hippocampus and the orbito-frontal cortex work in conjunction to send signals to the amygdala in the face of a perceived threat. This allows us to determine how significant the threat truly is. The orbito-frontal cortex does not complete its development until well into the twenty-fifth year of life. That is not a typo. This control center really is not fully developed until a child, or adult in this instance, is twenty-five years old. It seems that only the rental car companies have effectively embraced this concept. You cannot rent a car until you are in your early to mid-twenties. This makes sense considering that a young adult's brain is not fully developed up to this point. It is also interesting to note that this area of the brain is one of the few areas of the brain that remains open to influence throughout the lifespan.

The Regulatory System. The above discussion on the brain is a great segue to the regulatory system. When considering brain development from a contemporary perspective, one cannot discuss important areas of the social/emotional brain without also considering the regulatory system. Our regulatory system is, in fact, our stress response system. It is the system that becomes engaged in the face of stress, which helps us to manage the stress, interpret it, and respond accordingly. This area of human behavior has received more recognition in relation to human behavior during the last twenty years than any other area. One of the leading pioneers in the study of affect regulation is Allan Schore, Ph.D., a neuroscientist at UCLA. Dr. Schore has written three seminal texts on affect regulation, which have basically taken the work of John Bowlby, M.D., the father of attachment theory, and expanded upon it. According to Dr. Schore, so much of who we are and will ever become is established during our earliest regulatory relationships with our caregivers. Just as Bowlby stated that the first three years of life establish the blueprint for all of our future social and emotional relationships[8], Schore states, "The dyadic failure of affect regulation leads to the developmental psychopathology that underlies all later forming psychiatric disorders."[9] In other words, the failure of two people to create regulation together early in life is what leads to later forming psychiatric disorders. Stated even more simply, if you remain stressed for a long period of time and have no significant relationships to support you, you will become psychologically and emotionally impaired. Schore also states, "The core of the self is thus nonverbal and unconscious and it lies in patterns of affect regulation."[10] "It is not so much what you say or do, therefore, rather it is more important how you feel when you are doing or saying it."

Let's define two more important terms:

Regulation. Both regulation and dysregulation refer to our varying abilities to tolerate stress and to be in a state of stress. Regulation is the ability to experience and maintain stress within one's window of tolerance. Generally defined as being calm, this term is used throughout all sciences.

Dysregulation. Dysregulation is the experience of stress outside of your window of tolerance. This state is commonly referred to as being stressed out, or being in a state of distress. This experience is what scientists have consistently considered to be the attributing cause of eighty to ninety percent of most diseases and disorders. Other research has attributed nearly all psychopathology, which would certainly include reactive attachment disorder and oppositional defiant disorder, to affect dysregulation. We are all impacted by stress as we are all prone to shift from a regulated state into a dysregulated state and then, hopefully, back again. In general, it is our early regulatory interaction with our caregivers that determines our ability to regulate as we age. Alan Sroufe, another leading developmental neuroscientist, states, "Infants in well-regulated parental care systems become effective self-regulators in the face of stress as young children separate from the caregiver."[11] When an infant experiences a regulated environment, as this child grows older, he becomes increasingly more capable of tolerating stress when the parents are no longer present. This is particularly important during school, play, or time at the grandparents' home.

Unfortunately, as we will talk about in the next section, stress and trauma play havoc on our regulatory systems. In some instances, stress renders children literally unable to regulate, leading to an abundance of behavioral issues from lying, stealing, and hoarding to hyperactivity and aggression. **It is important to remember that children only act out in negative ways from a place of stress and fear.** Negative behavior is neither intentional nor planned without first the seeds of stress and fear – stress and fear which most likely has risen from an unconscious fear-based place.

The Impact of Stress and Trauma on the Social/Emotional Brain. It is important to understand that trauma can be any stressful event that is prolonged, overwhelming, or unpredictable. In this regard, most members of our society have experienced some degree of trauma. According to Candace Pert, author of *Molecules of Emotion*, following a traumatic event, if an individual does not have an opportunity to express, process, and understand the event to some degree in relationship with another human being, then any trauma can become stored within the cells of the body and have an impact on that individual for the rest of his life.[12] As you can imagine, most children do not have an opportunity to express, process, or understand why the things that happen to them have happened. So how do they communicate their pain? They communicate their pain through their behaviors – through behaviors which cannot be changed through consequences, logic, or control!

You may not always know what trauma your child has experienced or what event has caused him to be stressed. Though it can be important, it is not imperative. It is important because, as much as possible, you would want to be mindful and understanding if it occurred again, but not imperative because, with the correct understanding, you will be able to respond to your child as opposed to react, and that by itself can make a substantial difference.

Without going into a dissertation regarding the impact of stress and trauma on the brain, there are a few critical points to remember:

- Stress causes confused and distorted thinking and suppresses the short-term memory. When your child is stressed, he will not be thinking clearly, nor will he remember sufficiently from one situation to the next. Stress and trauma can impair the ability to communicate effectively between the left, thinking hemisphere of the brain, and the right, emotional hemisphere of the brain. In this regard, your child may feel angry, but not recognize that his body is in a state of fear. He may feel tired, but blame you for making him go to bed. Or during the midst of your upset with him over an incident, while you are angry and frowning, he may be smiling. He is not pushing your buttons as has been believed for years; rather he is not connected to his thinking and feeling. Only a crazy (please excuse the derogatory use of the term to make a point) person would laugh while someone is really angry. My point exactly! Your child is not crazy, but during high stress, he is disconnected from his thinking and feeling.

- Trauma impairs the ability to think clearly during stressful events. If you have ever wondered why your child is not learning at school, you might now consider that he is under too much stress to have a fully engaged thinking and memory system.
- Stress to a traumatized child may be life or death, while stress to you and me may simply be enjoyment and motivation. It has been said that there is a fine line between fear and excitement, joy and pain. Neurologically speaking, this is correct because both experiences arise from the amygdala, our fear receptor. Our memory system is what allows us to translate stress into joy or fear.
- Trauma creates a heightened stress receptor within the brain. In this manner, traumatized children will be more anxious, nervous, fearful, and subsequently, more aggressive.

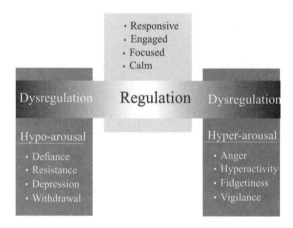

- According to Bruce Perry, nature equips us all to react to stress in one of two different ways: we either become hypo-aroused or hyper-aroused.[13] Hypo-arousal causes withdrawal, defiance, depression, and resistance. Hyper-arousal, on the other hand, causes hyperactivity, inattention, vigilance, and aggression. When a child or individual has experienced trauma, both reactions become heightened and more extreme.

For a more in-depth understanding of the impact of stress and trauma on the brain, there is a complete list of recommended readings at the back of this book.

CHAPTER THREE

The Patterns That Bind Us

■

"When patterns are broken, new worlds emerge."
– Tuli Kupferberg

PRINCIPLE #3
There is both Negative and Positive Repetitious Conditioning. We are all conditioned to behave in various ways both good and bad.

Children are conditioned to behave in the manner in which they do, both good and bad. To this same point, so are adults. We all essentially do the same thing because we have done it in this manner for so long. Our patterns of behavior are deeply woven into our cellular network. The popular evangelist Bishop T.D. Jakes said, "If you always do what you've always done, you will always be where you've already been." Such a statement is simple yet complex at the same time and speaks directly to principle number three.

As we attempt to learn something different, we must first recognize what we already know. If we fail to fully recognize what we already know, we may end up doing the same thing we have already done but just not realize that it is so. We want our children to behave differently, but we must also take on new behavior patterns. The only way to overcome a pattern of negative behavior which has become a conditioned reaction, is to counter it with a behavior pattern of positive response. For example, all of the behaviors that we will outline in this book have become patterns based on negative repetitious conditioning. Let's take lying, for example. Many children who have been diagnosed with reactive attachment disorder are notorious for their lying. Because these children typically lie out of fear, which in its presentation can look controlling and manipulative, we react to these children from fear. We do this by threatening; attempting to manipulate or control them back. A few examples include: "Tell me the truth or else," "I can see that you are choosing not to be honest; you'll need some time to think this through in your room," "If I can't trust you, I know you won't trust me, so I'm telling you now that you'll not have any dessert with us after dinner. Now you don't have to worry."

In these situations , the negative repetitious conditioning has already begun and we do not even realize it. We, the adults, are the cause of this negative conditioning, and we do not recognize it because we do not understand our child's fear, nor do we understand our own. The moment we react to our child's lie with some statement that lacks empathy, understanding, and support that we've pulled out of a book, we are simply reinforcing our child's need to lie again, but to do it better next time. When this happens day after day, twenty times a day, guess who becomes the master at lying? Practice makes perfect in this situation.

In order to overcome the negative conditioning, we must counter it with positive, repetitious conditioning. In this manner, because we understand that our child is conditioned, we should not expect him to not lie, but rather to lie very well. We then just hope that we notice him lying for a time or two, in an effort to implement some positive repetitious conditioning. So we wait. And we wait, not in an effort to "catch" him as in winning a battle, but we wait to help him. When we are certain that he is telling a lie, the behavior we are expecting because we now understand negative repetitious conditioning, we respond in a positive way as opposed to a negative. (We will discuss lying thoroughly in a later chapter – right now just focus on the understanding.) This one act has gone far in helping parents to help children stop lying. To respond to a negative with a positive eventually makes that negative a positive. The significance is that we understand the dynamics of conditioning and that it will be a process as opposed to an outcome. The outcome may arrive much quicker than expected; nevertheless, we are focusing on the process and not the outcome. If we understand the concept of conditioning, we can trust the process, which keeps us from perpetually fearing a negative outcome.

I believe one of the single best things I have ever said to a parent was: "Expect to fail." I encourage families to go home and fail just as soon as possible. Let me explain why.

You are not going to be perfect, but that should not stop you from trying. Expect to fail. But when you do, celebrate your failure because only then do you have an opportunity to learn and grow. Apologize to your child for your failure and vow to do better next time. As you practice the techniques and understanding that you will acquire from this book, do not expect your child to suddenly stop lying or stealing. Though it is highly possible, do not expect it. Expect your child to do the same thing he has always done, but you must commit to doing something differently. Soon your child will begin to experience positive, repetitious conditioning. This repetitious experience will eventually overcome the negative conditioning.

CHAPTER FOUR

Hidden Feedback Loops

■

"A soft answer turns away wrath."

– Proverbs 15:1

PRINCIPLE #4
Negative and positive neurophysiologic feedback loops exist beyond our conscious awareness. They occur at an unconscious physiologic level and we have the ability to change or add to these feedback loops.

In life there are two realities: the visible and the non-visible. Up until the past twenty years, we have not fully appreciated or been able to comprehend the significance of this reality. The study of neurophysiology has done much in assisting us to achieve a deeper understanding of our nonverbal, unconscious interactions with one another.

According to Allan Schore, "When a psychobiologically attuned dyad co-creates a resonant context within an attachment transaction, the behavioral manifestation of each partner's internal state is monitored by the other, and this results in the coupling between the output of one partner's loop and in the input of the other's to form a larger feedback configuration and an amplification of the positive state in both."[1] In other words, there is a fast-paced physiologic experience that occurs at the unconscious, non-visible level between two people. This is especially important between parents and children. Consider that 80% of communication is non-verbal. I am not sure that anyone knows exactly from what research this statement originated; nevertheless, it speaks directly to the feedback loops which occur between two people. It is estimated that if we could see with the eye the total sum of what two cellular systems engage in through vibratory interaction between one another, we would be overwhelmed by the information being processed. To make this very simple, anytime you engage with your child in any way, there is a physiologic communication process occurring called a feedback loop. There are two types of loops: negative and positive.

Have you ever walked up to a person who was smiling but obviously not feeling well, asked him how he was doing and he replied with, "Oh, I'm fine." Yet, all the while, you felt something otherwise? This is an example of a feedback loop. The response you received was in direct conflict with the energy being emitted from that person. This energy was the physiologic communication saying, "I'm not well at all."

As it applies to a family, another instance of a feedback loop is when a parent and all the kids are sitting at home feeling rather relaxed and the other parent pulls into the driveway. No one says anything, but everyone in the home begins to feel more tense, scared, or anxious. Suddenly, the child who was previously sitting, coloring a picture, is bouncing off the walls, being disobedient and completely defiant. This is a feedback loop.

When it comes to a feedback loop, we all have the ability to add to it or change it. It is an unspoken experience. Yet, with some degree of awareness and mindfulness, we can gain control over our environment. It must be understood at this point that, whereas traditional attachment and behavioral therapy approaches convey that the parent *must be in control*, we have failed to understand the true meaning of control. Control is the ability to influence the behavior of another individual as opposed to seeking to overpower or change his behavior. The only time we *seek* to be in control of another individual is when we feel threatened or fearful about some aspect of ourselves. When we are in a regulated state, there is no need to seek to be *in control* because, in this regulated state, control comes naturally and flows rhythmically with the interaction at the moment.

> ■
>
> *When it comes to a feedback loop, we all have the ability to add to it or change it. It is an unspoken experience.*
>
> ■

An example to illustrate control in the midst of both negative and positive feedback loops is the following:

A teenage child requests to go to a friend's house for a party with other friends, where there will be no adult supervision. For the child who has previous experience with her parents making wise choices, the thought of making this request will create a heightened stress sensitivity at the outset of the question. Hence, negative feedback has already been communicated before a single word is spoken. When the child asks if she may go to the party, the parent knows there is no possible way he would ever let this child – the one prone to acting out – go. The parent automatically reacts with mock sarcasm: "There is no possible way I am going to let you go to that party. There is no adult supervision. I don't know the parents of any of those kids there. I wonder, in fact, if their parents are even aware of what is going down. There will probably be alcohol there, too. I can't believe that you would even ask me that question. Are you nuts?" As you can guess, a negative feedback loop has been set in place. The teen exclaims to the parent that she is going regardless and that she does not think her dad is right, and in fact, her dad is being completely unfair. She protests that her father is being overly protective and does not ever understand a single thing about the teen. At this point the teen heads for the door. As is common, the father feels disrespected, slighted, embarrassed, ignored, and then hears the voice of his own parent yelling, "You will not disrespect me in my home, young man." A reflection from his own experience growing up, stemming from the state level of memory driving him to stand in front of the door, compels him to exclaim in much the same way his father did to him at this age: "You are not going out the door, young lady; furthermore, you will not talk to me in that manner while living in my house."

Not only is a negative feedback loop being established, but also it is compounded by the father's fear of losing his daughter and losing control of his home at the same time. He steps in to "regain control."

If you have ever experienced anything even remotely similar, then you know exactly how things are going to end. If the teen does not fight the father to leave the house, she walks away hating him and goes to her room in veiled resentment. She goes to her room under the assumption that she is staying home, pretending to her father that she is being compliant. Then, she sneaks out the window, only to come home drunk to a very angry and vengeful feeling father.

Negative feedback loops disempower the individual and create an emotionally overwhelming scenario. In this example, the father was moved into fear-based control and added to the feedback loop as opposed to changing it.

Let's look at the other scenario.

A similar situation occurs with the same teen and the same father. It just so happens to be two weeks later, after the father has thoroughly read and studied this book several times. Equipped with his new sense of empowerment in his own life, he is prepared for the presenting challenge. His daughter makes a similar request to go out to another party. Again, she expects a 'no' response with a greater degree of authority from her father, considering the way it worked out last time. Essentially, she is prepared for a fight and dead set on having it work out in her favor. Upon hearing the daughter's request, rather than reacting immediately with a 'no', the father takes a deep breath, reflecting on the situation that she is presenting him, and says the following to his daughter: "Honey, you are 15 years old and probably feel as though you are perfectly capable of making your own decisions. I can imagine that no matter what I say you are going to make the decision that you feel is best for you. I would like for you to stay home because I don't feel that the environment will be safe and I will worry about you tremendously. That being said, I know that you are going to do what you feel is best. I do love you though." Dad then turns and walks away.

He has just met a negative communication with a positive response, thereby creating an environment capable of containing the negative state being emitted from his daughter. A negative feedback loop cannot grow in the midst of a positive one. In addition, a positive feedback loop is capable of containing and ultimately changing a negative one. The father has just responded, rather than reacted, which then gives him the ultimate opportunity for influencing the outcome of the situation. Positive feedback loops empower.

The daughter, feeling completely dumbfounded by the answer and not quite knowing what to do, follows her father into the other room, thus moving further away from the door and further into the presence of the positive feedback. At this moment, Dad feels more powerful than he has ever felt before. He actually feels as though he has some control; but more than that, he is realizing that he is maintaining the relationship rather than losing the relationship by becoming scared, threatening, or controlling.

As Dad sits on the couch, his daughter comes into the room to say, "But may I go?" Dad reiterates his position feeling more confident with every passing second while, at the same time, giving his daughter control to make the best decision possible. She again is stopped in her tracks. In his audio tape series, *Emotional Intelligence*, Daniel Goleman states that the calmer amygdala has the ability to soothe the more dysregulated one.[2] In this instance, the father is practicing just this.

Feeling increasingly frustrated with herself, her father, and the situation, the teen proclaims that she is indeed going to the party. As she walks to the door, she is almost hesitant waiting for her father to demand that she stay home. He does not move. When she gets to the door, it is final; she will go and that is it. "Forget Dad," is her thought. Unfortunately, she cannot. He is not the threat. He is not trying to control her, but rather, he is supporting her to make the best possible decision. How could she possibly go against his wishes? She goes out the door. Naturally, the father is saddened, yet he feels somewhat hopeful. At least he has planted some seeds, and he does not feel nearly as guilty as he did just two weeks ago. He wrestles with the old messages: "Did she win? Am I being a pushover? Should I have demanded that she stay? Am I being a good father? Is this really what the book meant?"

The daughter walks to the driveway and tells her waiting friends that she is not going this time, turns and walks back into the house. Embarrassed, she closes the door and goes to her room. Suddenly, the realization sets in for Dad. It worked! He took charge, but in a different way. He was in control, but not in an ugly, degrading, and intimidating way. He thinks to himself, "Wow, this feels nice!"

Soon thereafter, Dad goes to his daughter's room and asks if she would like to share some ice cream. She agrees. He thanks her for staying home, and they enjoy the evening together.

Sound too easy? Maybe too good to be true? Maybe impossible with a child who has a trauma history? Sure it does, but it happened just like this between a mother and her sixteen year old son. It can work and often does, but we must realize the true power we hold in any situation is through influence, rather than through control. Rather than choosing to throw away our power as parents, we must embrace it and engage it from a non-threatening, responsive place.

In every behavior to be discussed throughout the following chapters, a feedback loop will be involved. The question is, "Are you going to change it or add to it?"

During a recent lecture, while discussing the four points we have just discussed, I asked the audience, "What do you call it when you do the same thing over and over while expecting a different outcome?" They replied, "Insanity." One mother in the audience exclaimed, "In our home we call that being stuck in stupid!"

So we invite you to read through the next chapters focusing on the specific behaviors in order to give you a new understanding that will empower you to connect with your children. This will create an environment in which your children can be emotionally regulated in order to connect with you. Additionally, there is a bonus section at the end that gives real-life stories from parents around the nation – real-life stories of how the Stress Model works in real-life situations with real-life children. Now, don't skip over the chapters and go straight to these stories. That is your fear driving you to the back of the book to see if this model really does work. Seriously, we encourage you to read each chapter thoroughly in order to gain a more comprehensive understanding, which will in turn, give you the tools you need to help your child and to develop a meaningful relationship with your child. Plus, the scenarios and stories in each chapter are real-life stories, as well, so you will see this model applied to real life throughout each chapter.

Congratulations! You have just finished reading the first four chapters of this book and are about to embark on Part II. In Part II, you will see the application of the four principles of the Stress Model as they relate to seven specific behaviors: lying, stealing, hoarding and gorging, aggression, defiance, lack of eye contact, and angry and hostile parents *(yes, there is even a chapter just for you, mom/dad!)*. In fact, instead of putting this chapter for parents at the end of this book as originally planned, we've moved it and it is the next chapter, just for you. We have to caution you, though: it tells a powerful story of how a child can open up deep wounds within the parent and how the parent can in turn be engulfed with rageful and hateful thoughts and feelings. It is not an easy chapter to read. Yet, it gives the truth and an understanding of what creates this dynamic and how to work through it as a parent or caregiver.

In each of the following chapters, you will see a "Quick Reference" at the end of each chapter, beginning with a Quick Reference for you on the Stress Model.

Quick Reference   **STRESS MODEL**

Principle #1: All negative behavior arises from an unconscious, fear-based state of stress.

Principle #2: There are only two primary emotions: Love and Fear.

Principle #3: There is both negative and positive repetitious conditioning. We are all conditioned to behave in various ways, both good and bad.

Principle #4: Negative and positive neurophysiologic feedback loops exist beyond our conscious awareness. They occur at an unconscious, physiologic level and we have the ability to change or add to these feedback loops.

- We first respond from our unconscious at the body level, before it is processed in our mind.
- This fear reaction then influences our ability to be responsive...fear sees problems and love sees solutions.
- The emotion of fear is the root of your child's anger...work to see your child as scared instead of angry.
- Children who are misbehaving are seeking external regulation.
- Behavior modification does not address a child's underlying stress.
- Traditional parenting techniques do not help a child learn to regulate through the parent-child relationship.
- Stress causes confused and distorted thinking.
- When parents are stressed, they are constricted and unable to open up to their child's emotional state.
- Positive repetitious experiences will eventually overcome negative conditioning.
- In the very moment when your child is misbehaving, he is doing the best he can to survive.
- Stress has an immediate impact on our unconscious mind triggering the following to occur:
    - living out of the past
    - avoiding the present
    - obsessing about the future

PART TWO

Seven Behaviors
Rooted in Fear

CHAPTER FIVE

Parents Appear Hostile and Angry

■

"Revenge is a confession of pain."
– Latin Proverb

While parenting can be tough and tiring work, most parents are able to sit back, take a deep breath, and reflect on the joys of parenting. Thoughts such as, "I love watching my kids learn and grow," "I love seeing her smile at me first thing in the morning," "I love having someone to hug who loves all the hugs I give," or "I love unsolicited kisses with no strings attached" easily come to mind for most parents. However, it is typical for parents with challenging children to reflect on the joys of parenting, and reflect, and reflect, and be completely void of such positive thoughts.

Parents dealing with extreme behaviors from their children often find themselves empty, depleted, and hopeless. They begin to regret their decision to parent, they begin to feel completely incompetent, and they begin to hate their role as a parent. Ultimately, they may even reach the point of "it's either him or me who has to go." After years of living with a child who is unable to reciprocate respect, affection, and love, parents go from being a lavish rainforest of love to an arid dry desert – hostile, angry, and depleted.

After seven long years of parenting an attachment challenged child, a mother came into my office one morning. Although she was a beautiful woman, she looked older than her years from the years of pain and power struggles. She was doubled over, crying in anguish to me, *"I can't do this anymore; I'm dying. I'm dying inside."*

Traditional View
Literature from the traditional view recognizes that parents of attachment challenged children often appear unreasonably angry.[1] The traditional view explains that these children have evolved into "masterful provocateurs,"[2] proficient at pushing their parents' buttons and arousing anger within the home.[3] Instead of engaging fully in family activities, these children watch the connections and interactions in order to identify these "buttons" to push later on when the time is right.[4] The traditional view further explains that due to this relentless provocation of anger, parents are truly victims of abuse within their own homes.[5]

This view explains that attachment challenged children purposely evoke this anger and that these children actually embrace their own negative behavioral acts.[6] Through these intense behaviors, they purposely create relationships filled with anger so the parent or caretaker will have no reason or desire to develop a relationship with them. This traditional view concludes that inducing anger, generating frustration, and creating distance is the child's principal goal.[7]

Parents giving advice to other parents from this traditional perspective often recommend that parents stay out of the "ick" by remaining detached from the child's controlling behaviors. Parents have been told by their therapists, "Every time they suck us in (we get mad, or yell, or show our annoyance), they get a zing."[8] Parenting advice by professionals reinforces this concept. Unconventional parenting techniques are said to be necessary for attachment challenged children in order to depersonalize the child's rebellion thus lowering the frustration level of parents.[9]

The key to success with these children, from this traditional view, is for parents to resist permitting the child to "activate" them. This model recognizes the difficulty for parents to stay out their anger, yet informs parents that this is the "family's only chance at succeeding."[10] Success will only be seen when the parent's anger decreases, which is an indication that the child is no longer "in control" of the parent's emotions. The child is no longer in charge; thus, the attachment between the child and parent will be able to build.

A New View
Parenting a child who, day in and day out, is defiant, lies, runs away, is aggressive, and/or is hyperactive, can be completely nerve grinding. In fact, the behaviors demonstrated by challenging children are just that: they are nerve grinding behaviors. The problem is that outsiders cannot see and cannot relate to just how ground-up the parents' nerves are becoming. The nerve grinding never ceases.

In an exploratory research study of adoptive mothers of children with special needs, it was found that 77 percent of the mothers either strongly agreed or agreed that since adopting, they experienced more rage and anger than ever before in their entire lives. One mother is quoted as saying, "I never had these feelings that I was capable of child abuse...just to feel this to such a degree is unnerving." The behaviors from their children became so nerve grinding that 14 percent of the mothers in the study had thoughts of suicide since adopting.[11]

While difficult and scary to admit, it is not uncommon for parents of attachment challenged children to reach such a heightened state of rage and hostility that they either have thoughts of killing themselves or killing their children. Such thoughts are frightening and unsettling for parents. It leaves them asking the question: "Where does this amount of rage come from?" To understand this parental reaction to a child's intense behaviors, we must revisit the concept outlined in Chapter 1 on the levels of memory. Four levels of memory were discussed: cognitive, emotional, motor, and state. It is in the state level of memory that trauma is stored and buried. Just as a child's early traumatic experiences are stored at the state level of memory, so too are the parents' earlier traumatic experiences.

In addition to the nerve grinding day-in-and-day-out of living with a child with severe behaviors, this child's emotional intensity works to "stir up" the parent's own past trauma history – trauma history of which the parent may not have even been aware. The parent's own state level of memory becomes activated at a deep unconscious level. Stephen Covey, in his national best seller, *The Seven Habits of Highly Effective People* says, "Upset feelings never die, they are buried alive and come back as something uglier."[12] Parents feeling intense amounts of rage are experiencing buried upset feelings that are essentially coming back as "something uglier."

To illustrate this, refer to the graphic of the file cabinet where each of the four drawers represents a memory state. The bottom drawer is the deepest level of memory, the state memory. This is where traumatic experiences that went unprocessed, unexpressed, and misunderstood are stored. Living with a child whose own behavior is driven out of this bottom drawer – a child driven out of a deep unconscious state of fear and overwhelm – eventually opens the parent's bottom drawer. The buried trauma within the parent is directly related to the rage that then surfaces within the parent.

An example of the opening of this bottom drawer is in the words below from a mother parenting a daughter that ignited intense internal feelings of rage, revenge, and hostility:

TRAUMA and MEMORY

Trauma is buried at the state level which directs all other responses.

I found myself being repelled by her mere presence. I couldn't stand to even be in the same room as my daughter. I hated her!

I had never in my life hated someone with such fervor. I found myself having thoughts of taking a knife and repeatedly stabbing her. One day while driving down the highway, I honestly wanted to just open the door while driving at 70 mph and push her out the door. As I imagined myself doing this, I felt no feeling of remorse, but rather revengeful feelings of justification and satisfaction. I often had feelings of wanting to beat her to an absolute pulp. As I would later reflect on these dreadful thoughts, I felt myself shift into a state of utter self-disgust, wanting to then end it all by killing myself. I was scared of myself and scared of my vengeful desires and thoughts.

As the quote says at the beginning of this chapter, "Revenge is a confession of pain." The revengeful thoughts written by this mother demonstrate the level of intense pain that can surface when parenting a child with deep traumatic wounds. For this mother, her daughter was uncovering years of buried pain and fear from her own childhood. Research on trauma experienced in childhood has shown that childhood exposure to trauma may not surface until it is triggered in adulthood. Symptoms from traumatic experiences can emerge months, years, or even decades after exposure to the traumatic event.

The fear-based reactionary parenting behavior that then surfaces is an internal safety response mechanism used to avoid activating the trauma memories. The parent's lack of resolution is maintained by cognitive and behavioral avoidance behaviors (anger and rage) that protect the core self from re-experiencing overwhelming feelings of fear and pain.[13] The anger and hostility serve to decrease intrusive experiences stored in the parent's memory,[14] thus decreasing the parent's ability to develop positive relationships.

For the mother in the above example, her daughter was an "associational connection" to her past experiences. "Associational connections may prime a link between memories of and ideas about a recent stressor event and those about a past trauma."[15] In his study to discern treatment strategies for traumatized children, Munson[16] found that, "caregivers of traumatized children are often themselves survivors of unresolved trauma and victims of repetitive compulsion, dissociation, and aloneness." In a pilot treatment study for traumatized children, the researchers acknowledged that, "this pain and distress is often unintentionally acted out onto the child by the wounded parent."[17] From this research, along with an understanding of the Stress Model, the traumatized child becomes the associational connection to the parent's unresolved trauma and loss issues, shifting the parent into a deep fear state.

The traditional view directs parents to stay out of their anger, but for many parents, staying out of this anger proves to be humanly impossible. The drive from the unconscious is so powerful that it can literally take parents hostage. No amount of self-talk, pre-determined action plans, or cognitive awareness can override these emotional outpourings.

From an understanding of the Stress Model, we can see that it is the stress-triggering event that is putting the parent in such an overwhelming fear-based state. It takes first an understanding of where the rage is coming from; it takes addressing the rage's origin, instead of addressing the rage itself. For some parents it may be as simple as taking a few deep breaths, breathing into the feelings of anger to identify connections to their own past experiences. For some parents, it may take journaling or meditation, creating a safe place for the unconscious fears to surface. Still, for other parents, it may take deep emotional therapy, such as psychosomatic therapy (therapy designed to activate the state level of memory at the body/mind level) to reach buried pain within the unconscious. Bruce Perry, M.D., remarks that, "You cannot change parts of the brain which are not activated. In order to change the 'state' you must activate the 'state'!" For many parents with buried and unresolved trauma, it takes much more than cognitive/behavioral therapy. It takes therapy that activates the state memory, allowing the unconscious to surface to a conscious level, along with opening up the body's sensory pathways.

■

Research on trauma experienced in childhood has shown that childhood exposure to trauma may not surface until it is triggered in adulthood.

■

No matter the method of addressing buried trauma, the "control" over this anger has to ultimately happen at the level of understanding. It is not simply controlling the anger through thoughts of "I have to stay in control over my child in order for my child to attach." It is not as easy as signing a contract in therapy about reducing the parent's anger towards her child.[18] Candace Pert, in *Molecules of Emotion*, proved through scientific research that emotions connected to painful, adverse experiences are stored deep within the cells of the body.[19] Thus, the dissipation of these emotions requires both thought and physical sensation. These stored molecules of emotions in the body/mind system cannot be controlled or maintained by cognitive thoughts or cognitive resolutions.

While it can feel as if the child is intentionally pressing the parent's buttons, it is a matter of the dynamics of trauma surfacing within the household. When the parent reacts out of fear, thus becoming more threatening to the child, the child then sinks deeper into his own fear state, opening that bottom drawer a little wider, and behaving more intensely. The parent, in turn, sinks into her own fear state, opening her bottom drawer a little wider, and reacting towards the child more intensely. Hence, the negative neurological feedback loop is in full swing and building as each person reacts and falls deeper and deeper into his/her own fear state.

In order to interrupt this negative neurological feedback loop, the parent has to recognize her own fear reactions and take ownership of her anger. The first question the parent needs to ask is, "Whose anger (fear) are we dealing with here?" The parent needs to find the courage to open up to her own emotional wounds in order to open up to her child's wounds. This can be an extremely scary place to enter. But if the parent is unwilling to address her own fears, the parent cannot expect the child to open up emotionally either.

As the parent is able to find healing, the parent will then be able to accept the child's pain and create an environment of emotional safety – where anger can be accepted and not taken personally. In doing so, the parent then shifts out of the traditional model of seeing the child pushing buttons; moves out of a place of seeing the child as purposefully creating tension in the relationship in order to keep the parent at a distance. Once the child is given permission to be angry and given the opportunity to be accepted in his anger, the defensive walls will begin to crumble. As the parent understands the associational connections being activated by the child's behaviors, the parent's own reactionary anger will subside automatically. The parent will no longer have a need to react, but will be in a place of love in order to be responsive and emotionally open to the child.

The mother continues her story:

> Once I realized the source of my anger and fear, I was able not only to change, but also to find healing from the deep wounds of my childhood. It wasn't about going back and blaming my parents or siblings, but simply understanding who I was and who I'd become as an adult. It was about honoring my fears, honoring myself in a way that allowed me to start living life out of a place of love, instead of being motivated from a place of fear. My daughter is truly a gift to me. She opened me up in areas that I had closed off under lock and key early in my life. The dark, internal pockets of emptiness, loneliness, and abandonment that I had denied and buried for years are now open. I'm alive and feel whole for the first time in my life! Now when my daughter's behaviors hit a sensitive nerve within me, I know that I don't have to react. I know that in this moment of emotional turmoil, she is only keeping me in

my process in order for me to be all that God has designed me to be.

This mother also realized that it was not that she had become a victim to her daughter, but that her daughter's behaviors were simply activating her own unresolved fears. The traditional view presents the issue of parental anger in a victimhood framework, correlating the extreme anger the children evoke within the parents to abuse – abuse by the children to their parents. In order to see this dynamic in a truthful and blameless perspective, we have to step outside of our own pain to see who is the wounded one in this situation. Certainly, the child is the one who has had the fear of others projected onto him in his past trauma experiences.

■

Living in a state of survival shifts us into parenting from a blame-based perspective.

■

When we get to the point of being frustrated and desperate, it is easy to slip into a fear-based place of seeing ourselves as the victim. Yet with the understanding presented above, the truth is that the parent has slipped into her own survival mode. She has felt so threatened in her own ability to remain sane and hopeful for the future that she goes into a self-protective stance. She fights back, fueled by the energy and fear unleashed by the triggers connected to her child's behaviors. She herself has now joined her child in living out of a place of survival.

Living in a state of survival shifts us into parenting from a blame-based perspective. Remember from the Stress Model that fear only sees problems; it cannot see solutions in the distortion it creates. So, the parent lives from a perspective of: "It's Johnny's fault. Our house wasn't like this prior to him being here. Our marriage certainly wasn't this bad before he brought his anger into this home!" When in this fear-based place, parents easily view their home as a prison where they are the prisoner. Driven by this fear, parents say to their children, "You have done everything you can to get out of this family. You have made me hate you."[20] The traditional view supports parents in seeing that the child is the source of this anger and that the child is the cause of this intense rage. Certainly these parents need to be first validated in their feelings, but then they need to be encouraged to reflect on their own past experiences that were buried – experiences that were unprocessed, unexpressed and essentially unfinished.

Parenting children with severe behaviors is not a simple job, yet it is a responsibility charged to us by God. It is a call to directly face our own fears, worries, and frustrations. Anytime those around us view our parenting struggles in a negative light, we are faced with the fear that perhaps we are not living up to the job bestowed upon us. Anytime we begin to feel as if we are ineffective parents, we are confronted with the fear of failing this calling. And anytime we see that we cannot help our children make better choices and begin fearing for our children's futures as teenagers or adults, we again slip into a place of fear. This only sends us spiraling downward into our own internal negative feedback loop.

Instead, we need to open ourselves up to the buttons being pushed within us by our children. Yes, let us go over that again. We need to open ourselves up to the buttons being pushed within us by our children. Children exhibiting severe behaviors present opportunities for us to find healing in places deep within the caverns of our hearts – dark places we never knew existed. They present us with the opportunity to make relational connections far greater than those known to mankind. While this may sound too poetic and dripping with sugar and icing to you, it is the perspective from which we need to work and strive to attain in order to ultimately relate to our children. When a parent's heart is open and operating out of a place of love, the parent has the emotional capacity to be in the child's pain with him, instead of reacting against the child's pain and against the child.

Continuing with this chapter's parenting story:

> *Once I realized the source of my anger and fear, I was able not only to change, but also to find healing from the deep wounds of my childhood. It wasn't about going back and blaming my parents or siblings, but simply understanding who I was and who I'd become as an adult. It was about honoring my fears, honoring myself in a way that allowed me to start living life out of a place of love, instead of being motivated from a place of fear. My daughter is truly a gift to me. She opened me up in areas that I had closed off under lock and key early in my life. The dark, internal pockets of emptiness, loneliness, and abandonment that I had denied and buried for years are now open. I'm alive and feel whole for the first time in my life! Now when my daughter's behaviors hit a sensitive nerve within me, I know that I don't have to react. I know that in this moment of emotional turmoil, she is only keeping me in my process in order for me to be all that God has designed me to be.*

Parenting Example – Parents Appear Hostile and Angry

Scenario: Beth is the mother of a defiant and rebellious 12 year old birth child named Rachel. Rachel has been a difficult child since she was an infant – hard to soothe, difficult to interact with, and often cold and aloof. Rachel's delivery was difficult and following birth, Rachel was colicky for the first two years of her life. Presently, Beth states that she is constantly angry with Rachel and that her relationship with her daughter is filled with tension, arguments, and power struggles. Beth admits that at this point, she has difficulty merely hugging her daughter and being in the same room with her.

Traditional View

From the traditional view, it can be seen that Rachel's early years of being colicky have created an attachment break in the parent/ child relationship. It is critical that Beth gain control over Rachel prior to Rachel becoming a full-blown teenager and, eventually, an adult. Notorious examples, such as Ted Bundy, have shown that even birth children who experienced breaks with their parents due to medical issues have the potential for growing up to be criminals.[21] Beth needs to see that Rachel is maintaining control in this relationship by keeping her mother angry, and she has been doing quite a good job at it for 12 years! Beth's first and primary objective needs to be to not let Rachel provoke her into anger. Beth needs to understand that every time Rachel is able to inflame her, Rachel wins control in the relationship. In order for Beth to lower her frustration, she must depersonalize herself from Rachel's behaviors – Rachel's behaviors are no longer Beth's responsibility. The onus is on Rachel, not Beth. In order for Rachel's behaviors to be central, distractions of anger from Beth need to be eliminated. In doing this, Rachel will be given the opportunity to understand that she cannot push her mother away with her power struggles. Her arguments will prove to be useless in activating her mother. Thus, Beth commits to changing her reactions to Rachel's behaviors. She wakes up every morning and repeats her mantra of, "I'm in charge; Rachel does not have the power to make me angry today." However, after two months of working hard not to react, Beth finds herself time and time again, slipping into complete anger against Rachel. Even when Beth is able to control her outbursts, she finds herself unhappy and lacking the desire to engage with her daughter. Beth talks to her therapist and her therapist encourages Beth to simply work harder to stay in control, avoid getting "zinged," and avoid a control battle, emphasizing that Beth *must* win.[22] The therapist reminds Beth that these must be accomplished in order for her to be able to reach her daughter.

A New View

Implementing the Stress Model, Beth realizes that the intense anger she is experiencing is being driven from an unconscious place within her. At this point, it is about Beth, not Rachel. The onus is on Beth to identify the source of her over-reactions to her daughter. The next time Rachel acts out and Beth feels herself about to react in anger, Beth steps back, sits down, takes a deep breath, and says to herself, "I'm scared." Beth realizes that in doing this, she is speaking to the unconscious fear within her. Yet, Beth feels herself getting even angrier by stepping back. She continues breathing and realizes that her body literally feels like it is on fire at this point and she feels as if there is an emotional tornado swirling within her. Beth tells her daughter that she is going to her room for her own parental time-out, being mindful to break the negative feedback loop. Later that evening, once Rachel is in bed, Beth sits down at the computer. She begins breathing, closes her eyes, and begins typing the thoughts that surface. By closing off her visual sensory pathway, Beth is making space for her unconscious thoughts to surface. After a time of typing random thoughts, she types, "My sister would always have to have the last word." Beth opens her eyes and exclaims out loud, "That's it! That's it!!!" Beth realizes that growing up with two alcoholic parents, she would always back down from arguments with her sister in order to keep peace in the home. Beth's parents could not handle outward expressions of anger. Beth realizes that now, as an adult, she is re-enacting those moments. Yet, this time around, Beth is going to have the last word. When her daughter argues with her, she is really seeing her sister. Being driven out of a state of fear in order to ensure that she is finally going to be acknowledged and heard, Beth ignites into a rage-filled state with Rachel. Beth makes this associational connection so that the next time Rachel enters into an argument or talks back to her, Beth can acknowledge her unconscious desire to have the last word, which will then enable her to shift into a state of love with Rachel. She can then remain present with Rachel, without having to control her. As Rachel feels heard, her need to argue and set power struggles into motion will decrease.

Quick Reference **PARENTS APPEAR HOSTILE AND ANGRY**

Remember that being hostile and angry as a parent is:
- A sign of being worn down by "nerve-grinding" behaviors.
- Typical for parents dealing with attachment challenged children.
- An indication of the parent's dormant trauma memories being awakened.
- A symptom of the parent's own "unfinished business."
- A protective device as hostility and anger are internal safety responses working to avoid the activation of painful memories.
- An indication that the parent is acting out of fear and shifting to a blame-based posture.

When feeling angry and hostile, recognize that your child needs you to:
- Understand that you are not the victim; rather that both of you are experiencing raw and painful emotions of fear.
- Know that he is not purposely working to make you angry.
- Take ownership of your internal reactions. Open yourself up to the wounds that trigger your feelings.
- Understand that your anger and hostility is threatening and sends him into a deeper fear state.
- Confront your own fears in order for you to help him confront his fears.
- Find healing for yourself first in order to then open the pathway for his healing.

CHAPTER SIX

Lying
∎

"Lying to ourselves is more deeply ingrained than lying to others."
– Fyodor Mikhailovich Dostoevsky

"**W**hat kind of people chronically lie?" The most common answers are: (a) car salesmen, (b) con men, (c) criminals, (d) adulterers, (e) thieves, and, yes, (f) lawyers. When our children lie to us, we fear they will grow-up to be dishonest adults. Within a millisecond of our child lying to us, we panic and envision a lifetime of our child lying to people, creating havoc in relationships, getting fired from jobs, and maybe even doing time in jail.

As parents, lying is a difficult behavior to address in our children for two primary reasons. First, lying is difficult because of the fear we project into the future for our child. We fear our child will not have a strong moral base as an adult, which will ultimately affect his relationships, his employment, and his overall ability to succeed in life. Second, lying is difficult because of our own discomfort from past experiences of people lying to us. When we as parents experience our child lying, it can be like getting swallowed up into a time machine and re-experiencing a painful lie of the past. Yet this time around, we experience the lie on the big screen in full technicolor. We experience the discomfort within ourselves, target our child as the cause of our discomfort, and immediately begin reacting in order to change our child's behavior, unconsciously thinking: "If I can stop you from lying, I can stop my own discomfort."

Recently, when a mother began discussing a situation involving her son with me during a small parenting workshop, she expressed pure frustration about her eight year old son's lying behavior. With stern conviction, she stated, "My son has got to learn that lying is morally wrong. He needs to be taught a lesson now before he grows up. Lying is wrong and will not be tolerated in my home." Do you hear the fear in those words? After supporting her reaction and validating her, I asked her, "Who lied to you as a child?" Such a deep-seated emotional reaction expressed in her words and her tone of voice was only stemming from a place of darkness within herself. It was stemming from an unprocessed and hurtful experience, or experiences, stored in her deepest level of memory. It was coming from her state level of memory. After the initial shock of my shifting

" the focus off of her son and onto her, she took a deep breath and said, "My father lied to me." Encouraging her, I sat down on my stool and said, "How bad was it? Tell me more." She replied, "I was about eight years old and the fighting between my mother and father had escalated into physical violence. My father sat all of us kids down in our formal dining room for dinner and emphatically stated, 'We're not getting a divorce.'" As tears welled up in her eyes, she said, "Three weeks later my father left our home, divorced my mother, and never stepped foot in our home again." Emotional reactivity stems from unfinished business. The associational connection between her son being eight years old presently and her being eight years old previously was a prevalent aspect of her reactivity to her son's lying behavior.

Attachment-challenged children commonly exhibit lying behaviors, and not only do they exhibit chronic lying, but they also often exhibit nonsense lying. This lying behavior can occur several times during a single day. Day after day of dealing with this type of lying behavior can drive even the most patient parent into rage-filled behaviors. First, let us look at how traditional therapists view this behavior and what advice they give to parents. Second, let us look at this behavior through the understanding of the Stress Model and what the application of this understanding would be for parents working to create a healing environment within their homes.

Traditional View

Traditionally, attachment therapists view lying as a way for children with trauma histories to take control. Lying develops into a habitual strategy in order to gain power and control, and certainly as a way to avoid punishment.[1] It is viewed as a way for the child to distort the parent's world and as a way to turn the parent's world into utter confusion. Lying is seen as a way for the child to impose the chaos in his own brain onto someone else who he wants to hurt. It is seen as a way for the child to "test" the parent child relationship. By lying, the child is pushing the adoptive parents or the foster parents to their breaking point in order to see if they *really* mean that they are his parents always.

This view explains that attachment-challenged children do not trust and, therefore, react from a place of distrust in order to then gain the ability to trust. Lying is seen as a patterned behavior that needs to be reprogrammed through consequences and that parents need to "beat the child to the punch" in his lying behaviors. Some traditional views go as far as to say that these children are born liars.[2] Others create fear by describing lying as a "hallmark sign of anti-social children."[3]

Traditional attachment therapists' recommendations based upon these interpretations of lying focus on the goal of not allowing the child to use the lie to control the parents. Advice is commonly given for parents to say, "I don't believe you" to the child after he tells a lie.[4] The explanation is that this statement diminishes the controlling effect the child is working to obtain through the lie. Parents are told to tell their child, "I can love you no matter what you have done or have had happen to you. How long do you think you need to keep up your lying behaviors until you figure that out?" Parents are also told to be one step ahead of the child by saying, "I want to talk to you and I know you don't tend to tell the truth when I ask you questions. So, I want you to know I expect you to come up with a really good lie to answer my question. Ready?" The goal of such statements is to put the child in conflict about his lying.[5]

Under this understanding of the attachment challenged child, parents are told that the child must not experience the parent angry or emotionally triggered by the child's lie. The advice is that the child needs to feel and experience emptiness as a result of his behavior. Negative consequences are also encouraged as a way for the lesson of lying to be experienced by the pain of a consequence. Attachment-challenged children are not viewed as children who can simply think through the pain they have caused others by their lying and, therefore, they need a negative consequence to actually experience the pain of their lying.[6]

A New View

Research in the field of neuro-science has shown that children who have experienced trauma react to stress out of a state of fear, from an unconscious level, as deep as the state memory. The fear receptor in the brain becomes overly triggered and, in this stress state, the traumatized child's perception of the situation at hand becomes distorted and exceptionally fearful.

Children with trauma histories are living out of a primal state of survival. They literally lie from a place of life or death. Their survival is dependent on convincing you that they are telling the truth. In this distortion of their mind, the state level of memory drives them with the conviction that they must persist with this lie at all costs in order to survive.

Simple events throughout the child's day can cause intense fear reactions. It can be as simple as a child picking up a penny off of the floor belonging to someone else and lying about it. It can be as obvious as a child hitting his sister and denying it, even after the parent witnessed the behavior. It can be as absurd as lying about stealing a pencil off of the teacher's desk while standing in front of the teacher, holding the pencil in hand. This type of lying can be absolutely maddening for the parents (caretaker, teacher, etc). Parents soon begin to question their own sanity when living with this type of behavior; the child's lying challenges their own reality.

In order to understand this lying behavior, we must first acknowledge that the child is simply reacting from a state of fear. It is critical that we acknowledge that when children with trauma histories are triggered into their stress and confronted in a lie, they will continue to reinforce the lie. Thus, the awareness that the child's unconscious is saying, "I have to convince you I'm telling the truth because my life depends on it" is necessary in order for the parent to respond from a place of love, instead of a place of fear and punishment.

It is vital for parents to identify their own reactions first.

Thus, the ability for the parent to help the child depends on the parent's ability to avoid buying into the lie. This is an extremely difficult task because lying is a threatening behavior. When our children lie to us, it causes a stress reaction in our brain – a stress reaction within our body-mind system. We then go into a hyperaroused state and say to the child, "Now, tell me the truth. You're lying to me. I've told you more than a hundred times not to lie to me." Yet, as soon as we do this, we have only fed into their fear and increased their determination to convince us of the lie. Parent and child then enter into a negative feedback loop, each driving more fear into the other.

So the question is then, "Can you as the parent ignore the lie?" If you immediately say, "No, I can't do this," recognize this as a rigid reaction. And then the question becomes, "Well, who lied to you?" Someone must have lied to you to have such a strong reaction. When your child lies to you, it puts you into an emotionally reactive state. Remember that emotional reactivity stems from our own unfinished business. Ask yourself, "Is this emotionally charged response stemming from something in my own history?"

It is vital for parents to identify their own reactions, first. Otherwise, the parents will not be in a calm place physiologically or emotionally to help their child. Scientific research shows that within an interaction between two people, the person with the calmer amygdala (the fear receptor in the brain) has the ability to soothe the one that is activated. (Refer to Chapters 1 through 4 for a review of this information). This translates to an understanding that the parent must be regulated in order to calm the child.

So it becomes critical with this understanding for the parents not to buy into the lie in order to maintain a calm state, a state that does not allow their own amygdala to get triggered. It is then that the parents are able to create a different physiological environment for their child. They can then work to help calm the child by embracing their child with a hug and calmly saying, "You're not going anywhere. Everything is going to be okay, sweetheart."

Doing this can have a dramatic impact on the child's state level of memory. By doing this, the parent is addressing the child's unconscious fear, while calming the child through the sensory pathways (sight, sound, and touch).

But you're saying by this point, "Okay, calm the stress...I get that. But what about the fact that my child is lying? How is he going to know that lying is wrong?" You are absolutely right; lying is wrong and the moral lesson of lying should be taught...it just cannot be taught in the heat of the moment due to the child's fear reactivity. Once the child is calm, and you're calm, perhaps in an hour or later in the day, this behavior can be addressed with the child. Yet, in order for the child to absorb and fully understand that lying is wrong, the child has to be out of his fear state. His cognitive thinking pathways have to be clear and open. These pathways are engaged and fully operational only when a child is in a state of love. Remember, stress causes confused and distorted thinking, so the child must be in a calm state in order to be receptive to the rationale of why it is hurtful to lie.

It is also important to recognize that stress suppresses short-term memory. Lecturing a child about lying during the stress of the moment will have little impact on the child's ability to remember not to lie in the future. Consequencing the child during the act of lying with statements such as, "Your TV privileges will be removed if you continue to lie to me" or "You're not getting dessert tonight if you don't fess up to lying to me," will only heighten the child's stress level, creating more confusion and distortion. These fear-based demands prolong and heighten the child's fear, preventing the child from being able to remember the life lesson the next time he is confronted with a stressful situation. He will not be able to remember that he received consequences for lying in the past. His short-term memory will not allow him to remember.

It takes positive interactions and a positive environment to calm a child's reactive stress state.

So the formula for lying behavior states: "Ignore the lie, but don't ignore the child." The goal is to establish a dynamic that creates true regulation through the parent-child relationship. As the child experiences more and more positive responses from the parent, this regulating relationship between parent and child will permeate the state memory, lessening the reactivity of the child's stress response system. This will, in time, decrease the child's need to lie to the parent. It takes positive interactions and a positive environment to calm a child's reactive stress state. And it takes repetition of both the positive relationship and repetition of the positive environment to create long-term healing for the child.

Parenting Example: Lying

Scenario: As the family is getting ready in the morning, Mom asks, "Suzie, did you feed the cat and give him fresh water?" Abruptly, Suzie says, "Yes." Mom looks over at the cat's bowl and sees that there is no food and sees that there is only a small amount of stale water in the bowl.

Traditional View

Suzie is trying to control her mother at this point in the morning because earlier Suzie had asked her mother to make pancakes and her mother said no. Additionally, since her mother wouldn't make her pancakes, Suzie is fearful that her mother does not really love her and Suzie is using the situation to test her mother. In order for Suzie's lie to lose its effectiveness and ability to control the situation, Suzie's mother needs to calmly say, "I know you're lying because the food dish is empty. I love you always; it is up to you to decide when you are going to believe me and believe that I am your mother and that I will never leave you." This absurd lie was a conscious choice on Suzie's part and the parent must not emotionally react to the lie; otherwise, a reaction from Mom would empower Suzie, only reinforcing this type of controlling behavior.[7]

A New View

Suzie is upset and stressed about the earlier interaction with her mother regarding the pancakes. Suzie's state memory became activated and fear-based unconscious thoughts begin to surface: "If she won't make me pancakes, how do I know that the next time I'm hungry, I'll get fed? And if I don't get fed, I'll die. I've got to make sure I'm a good girl – that I'm perfect in order for my mom to take care of me." Suzie's immediate response of "yes" when asked about her morning chore did not have time to be processed in the cognitive mind. It was an automatic reaction from her state memory in order to ensure her survival. If she does exactly what her mother has asked her to do, if she is the perfect child, she'll survive; she'll be okay. Mom needs to respond to Suzie's fear by holding her hand, placing Suzie in her lap, and saying, "Suzie, I love you. You're going to be okay and nothing can stop me from taking care of you." Later that day, when Suzie is calm, Mom can sit and talk to Suzie, touching or holding her gently. Mom can then say, "Suzie, it hurts me when you lie to me. Sometimes when we get scared, we lie to one another. I want you to know that I love you and you're not going anywhere. I'm here to always take care of you. You can always tell me the truth, honey."

Quick Reference   **LYING**

Remember that lying:
- Comes from a state of survival – the child must persist with the lie at all costs in order to survive.
- Easily creates a fear reaction in the parent.
- Is a fear-based behavior; a threatening reaction from the parent only feeds into the child's fear.

When finding your child in a lie, recognize that:
- Lying stems from a state of stress.
- The lying behavior is not directed at you personally.
- Your child is reacting from past trauma experiences.
- Your child already feels threatened, so confronting the lie will only heighten and create more threat.
- Your best response is to "ignore the lie, but not to ignore the child."
- Your child cannot be taught the moral lesson of lying while in the act of lying.
- Your child's foundation is insecure and your child needs your help in building the parent/child relationship through a nonblaming, non-punitive environment.

CHAPTER SEVEN

Stealing

∎

*"Ordinary riches can be stolen, real riches cannot. In your soul
are infinitely precious things that cannot be taken from you."*
– Oscar Wilde

Stealing is a behavior that goes against our American culture of working hard for what we have. Stealing is counter to one of the foundational principles our country was built upon – that of private ownership. As Americans, we treasure the right to own property and the right to be respected for what we own. When a possession is stolen from us, we feel personally violated. And if something personal is stolen from us – right within our home by our very own child – it evokes a bodily/emotional response within us that goes beyond fingernails being scratched on a chalkboard.

Attachment-challenged children commonly exhibit stealing behaviors. These stealing behaviors can range from stealing from stores to stealing from teachers to stealing from family members, or all of the above. Many times, the items stolen have little or no meaning to the child, leaving parents perplexed as to why the child stole the items and how to handle the situation. The stealing can also happen several times, not only within one day, but repeatedly within an hour's time.

A mother of a child with a severe trauma history described a situation with her son to me. The child, Danny, was caught at school stealing pencils off of his teacher's desk. On this occasion, the child was taken to the principal's office, as this had been a perpetual behavior of this child. The child was regretful, made an apology to the teacher and principal, and spoke with his mother on the phone, admitting to the theft and pleading for her forgiveness. Upon returning Danny to his classroom, he then stole another item right off of the teacher's desk, not more than five minutes after being back in his classroom. The mother, with a perplexed look on her face, was beyond feeling frustrated, and was simply dumbfounded by her son's actions.

Traditional View

Traditional attachment therapists view stealing as an effective tool for children because it puts parents into an intense level of frustration, thus putting the child in a "winning position."[1] Stealing is seen as a sign that the child cannot be trusted in the home or at school. Due to the fact that much of the stealing is irrational and involves stealing of insignificant items, it is seen as a passive-aggressive technique for these children. These passive aggressive acts become a sure way for children to gain control and manipulate their parents and teachers.[2]

Stealing is thus seen as a way for the child to exhibit power and control over those in authority. In order to minimize this behavior, parents are given the advice to assume the child is guilty until proven innocent and to assume that the stealing behavior is the child's *modus operandi*. Parents can then take charge of the behavior by saying, "I don't believe you did not steal my calculator. You will have to pay for the calculator now and if it shows up later, I'll do everything to make it up to you then."[3] This type of consequencing is seen as essential to the parent staying in control and for the child to learn to develop respect towards other people's property. Parents are told that children who steal should not be permitted to borrow things from others and should not be allowed to accept "undeserved" gifts.[4] This keeps the parent one step ahead of the child, thus, preventing the child from claiming that the stolen item was given to him.

Stealing can also be interpreted as a way for children to fill the empty holes in their hearts.[5] Professionals further explain that this behavior develops when these children see other children happy, so they attempt to "steal" this happiness for themselves. Thus, they actually think they can rip off happiness to fill their chronic emptiness.[6]

A New View

Children with trauma histories are typically poor self-regulators. Children who have grown-up in violent, punitive, neglectful, fearful environments, devoid of sufficient regulatory figures (parents who have been unavailable and unable to calm and pacify the child during times of stress), have regulatory systems that are ineffective at calming internal stressful states. Their regulatory development has been interrupted and has gone awry in its attempt to compensate for the lack of external calming – external calming from a parent figure that they are biologically designed to receive. In order to comprehend fully a child's "non-sense" stealing behaviors, the understanding and application of this insufficient regulatory system is critical.

If a child has difficulty regulating himself internally, the body will automatically seek to calm this stress externally. Thus, stealing is an external attempt at soothing an internal state of dysregulation, similar to other addictive behaviors such as smoking, alcoholism, and even eating chocolate. The body reacts at a physiological level when engaged in addictive behaviors, which enables the body to regulate for a moment of time. An identical reaction occurs when a child steals. There is an enormous chemical reaction that takes place in the brain and body system that literally creates a rush or a release for the child, calming the child. For a hyper-aroused child, the act of stealing is similar to taking a suppressant, such as heroin. It calms the body down. For a hypo-aroused child, the act of stealing is similar to taking a stimulant, like cocaine. It gives the body a "rush" that puts the depressed and shutdown child into a state of alertness, which feels good for the child.

Stealing behavior can create the same rush for adults. A recent news story describes J. L. Hunter Rountree as America's oldest known bank robber. Formerly a tycoon who founded a Texas machinery company, Rountree pulled his first heist at the age of 86. When asked why he robbed banks, he replied, "It's fun. It feels good, awful good. It feels good for sometimes days, for sometimes hours."[7]

Children with trauma histories typically steal items that offer no physical or material payoff; it is not about being afraid of getting caught. They are simply acting out to seek a physiologic payoff. Once Joey puts that box of paperclips in his pocket from the office supply store, an immediate payoff within the body system is received. Yet, once he steals, the rush or suppressant is completely worn off in 5 minutes. Then, Joey experiences even more stress than before, leading to a continual need to steal. The addictive behavior begins its vicious cycle. Joey begins to steal repetitively, and his system begins to be conditioned to believe that all he has to do is put that pencil or piece of candy in his pocket and everything will be okay. It becomes a brutal cycle of finding a moment of regulation, followed by returning to a state of dysregulation.

Children will steal in certain environments as a reaction to certain stimuli. Mom takes Billy, an eight-year-old adopted child, into the local Wal-Mart. As you have experienced yourself, Wal-Mart is an overwhelming and stimulating environment for even the most regulated adult; and we won't even think about a Super Wal-Mart! For Billy, a child easily triggered into a stress reaction, just the thought of going to Wal-Mart pushes him into a dysregulated state. The responsible approach for Mom would be to help Billy understand what happens to him when he goes into this environment and to identify his unconscious drives through her verbal communication with him. So Mom says to her son prior to even leaving the house for the shopping trip, "Billy, when you get stressed out and you get scared, you have a tendency to stick things in your pocket that don't belong to you. The reason you do this is because when you stick something in your pocket, it makes you feel good. What I need you to understand is that when you feel scared and stressed out, you can come to me and let me know. And secondly, when you stick things in your pocket that don't belong to you, that really hurts and scares other people. When people have things stolen from them, they get angry – angry with you. What I want you to know is that I understand that when you get scared or stressed out, you steal things. We are going to Wal-Mart today and when we get into the store, I'm going to keep you next to me to keep you safe."

In such a case, it is even recommended to simply practice with the child, whether a young child or a teenager. Practice talking with the child, then go into the store, creating containment with either the child in the basket or next to you, with the child holding your hand. (Yes, even holding hands with your teenagers because they will know at an unconscious level that they feel safer with you.) Simply go up and down the aisles, maybe buy a treat to eat, and then go home – no shopping list, no agenda, nothing to lose the focus of helping your child to feel safe in the store.

Doing this will begin the process of helping your child to develop the ability to regulate by himself. He needs you to come to him in a non-punitive, compassionate way, taking responsibility for helping him understand and change his behavior. He needs you to come to him in a non-blaming way in order for his regulatory system to be given the "fertilizer" it needs to grow and develop. Your child will be learning to regulate through the safe relationship you create with him. In turn, he will then expand his ability to self-regulate. The body's natural ability to regulate will be given the opportunity to reconnect and realign through the safety you provide for your child.

Once a child is calm and feels safe, the human regulatory system has been shown to develop in a rapid period of time and has been seen to "catch-up" to its developmental potential. Within two weeks to thirty days, you will see a reduction in this type of behavior through mindful practice, and calm communication, and responsible parenting that is free of blame and free of punishment – parenting that is beyond consequences, logic, and control.

If a child is stealing from the home, the child is communicating to the parents that she cannot handle the stress in the home. The child needs you to create safety and containment because she is beyond her ability to stop this behavior on her own. Close the doors to the bedrooms and keep your child in a contained space as close to you as possible all the time. You have essentially created a smaller area, which is less threatening, and she no longer has the run of the house. Remember that when you see improvements in her behavior, the reason she is not stealing is because she is staying more regulated with you. She is connecting with you at a physiologic level. Emotionally, she is feeling safer and she is no longer feeling threatened.

At school, the child needs the same kind of responsible joining from the teacher and school staff. Ms. Jones says, "Billy, I know when you get stressed and scared in class, you feel like stealing from my desk. I want you to know that everything is going to be all right and I'm here to help you. The next time you feel like going to my desk and putting something in your pocket, I want you to let me know – just raise your hand and ask me to come over to your desk. You won't be punished, no time off of your recess, no infractions, no referrals. I just want to make sure you have someone to share your feelings with while in my classroom, so please let me help you."

Parenting Example: Stealing

Scenario: Sam, a fifth grader, comes home for the third day in a row with items that do not belong to him. This time he brings home a blank videotape from the media center and ketchup packets from the lunchroom. The days prior, he brought items that were useless to him from his music teacher and art teacher, as well as items from the cafeteria.

Traditional View
Sam is stealing items from outside of his regular classroom (music and art classes, the media center, and the cafeteria). Sam is using this behavior to set the tone for his need to control and for his complete disregard and disrespect for adults in this school. This stealing behavior is his attempt to control these unsuspecting teachers and to win in the power game between student and teacher. His mother needs to have a joint meeting with his music and art teachers, the librarian, the head cafeteria worker, and the principal, with Sam in attendance at this meeting. This meeting will demonstrate to Sam that all the adults are on the same team[8] and that his controlling behaviors and "tricks"[9] are futile. He will be reminded of all the past events to help him maintain more perspective of the present.[10] It will also be pointed out to him that he is out-numbered and out-powered, and needs to submit his control to those in charge.

A New View
Sam is stealing outside of his classroom because he is reacting to the stress created from transitioning from one class to another. Additionally, his consistent stealing from the cafeteria is a sign that this environment is overly stimulating for him and that he is stressed in this environment. Sam takes these insignificant and useless items in an attempt to soothe his internal stress state. He has not attempted to hide them from his mother because he is not stealing to "see what he can get away with," but simply using external items to help him deal with his feelings of fear and overwhelm during the transitional times at school. His mother needs to have a joint meeting with his music and art

teachers, His mother needs to have a joint meeting with his music and art teachers, the librarian, the head cafeteria worker, and the principal, with Sam in attendance at this meeting. In this meeting, Sam will sit close to his mother, and she will explain to him in a soft voice that each of these people are here at the school to help him. She will explain that when he begins to feel overwhelmed and stressed when transitioning, he has people to talk with and that these school personnel will take a more active role in helping Sam make the transition. Each person at the meeting will encourage Sam and reassure him that he is safe at school and that he is going to be okay.

Quick Reference   **STEALING**

Remember that stealing:
- Is an external attempt to soothe an internal state.
- Is an addictive behavior.
- Becomes repetitive because of the internal payoff. Repetition changes the brain so the stealing becomes a conditioned response to a stress state.

When discovering your child has stolen, recognize that he needs you to:
- Keep him close to you in that environment; limit his space and create containment for him.
- Explain to him the dynamics of the stealing behavior; communicate to him about why he steals and that stealing makes him feel better.
- Explain to him you are not coming from a blame-based perspective, but that you are coming from a place of taking responsibility for him.
- Address the root mechanisms that lead to the behaviors and reach him in the deep emotional place that drives this behavior.
- Teach him how to communicate to you when he feels like stealing, saying, "I need to know how you feel when you go into a store. Help me to understand."

CHAPTER EIGHT

Hoarding and Gorging

■

"The first duty of love is to listen."
– Paul Johannes Tillich

Food – what an interesting little word. It is a simple, quaint little word with quite complex applications. Not eating food can kill us, while eating certain foods can kill us, as well. We use food to meet our basic human needs, yet on the other end of the spectrum, food is much more to us than a basic ingredient to our survival. We use food to celebrate. We use food to decorate. We write about food. We animate food into cute cartoon characters. We cover billboards with pictures of food bigger than life. We dedicate entire television networks to food. We buy subscriptions to magazines devoted to food. We use food in religious ceremonies as symbols of sacrificial love. Fast food restaurants build playgrounds around serving food. Universities grant degrees in food. We build food museums. Megacorporations are created and built around food. Generations of farm families create entire family cultures around the growing of food. Marketing companies dress up food in bright colors and fancy packages. *And then our attachment-challenged child joins this bandwagon and uses food in ways we could never have imagined!*

It is typical for children with severe neglect and deep trauma histories to have issues around food. These food-related behaviors can include hoarding and gorging food. Many parents report that their child steals food from the kitchen or from school and stashes it in his bedroom. Other parents report children waking up in the middle of the night and going into the pantry, only to be found eating sugar, handful after handful. Parents often find candy wrappers stuffed behind the bed or in the child's closet – and not just one candy wrapper, but twenty or thirty wrappers, all wadded up in the corner.

A foster mother relates her story:

> *One day I was cleaning my son's room and found thirty empty soda cans in his laundry basket, ten more soda cans in his drawers, and another ten or more cans under his bed. Down to the refrigerator in the garage I go, only to find that all the soda that was kept cold there for the entire family was gone – every single can was gone!*

Traditional View

From the traditional view of the attachment-challenged child, eating and mealtime are seen as a control time for children. It is thought that these children use food as a direct point of conflict. They reject any semblance of appropriate eating behaviors in order to create conflict within the family system.[1] Mealtime is seen as a time to create this conflict, as mealtimes are a time for closeness and intimacy within the family. Thus, it is explained that attachment-challenged children do everything they can to be removed from this unspoken time of closeness.[2]

Children with attachment issues are viewed as controlling in the area of eating because providing food is a way for parents to provide nurturing at a very basic level for these children.[3] Nationally recognized attachment therapists have pointed out that many children go so far as to vomit at mealtime in order to avoid any nurturing from their parents.[4] Thus, these behaviors are viewed as a way for these children to reject this nurturing in order to stay in control and to stay in charge.

This traditional stance proposes that instead of receiving the nurturing from the parent, children hoard and gorge food to receive the nurturing – without the attachment figure present (as in the above example from the foster mother) – and they sneak behind closed doors and sneak around at night time to fulfill this natural need for comfort. These children are seen as eating in an attempt to fill a chronic emptiness inside[5] and it is explained they hoard sweet foods because this is the closest they can come to feeling loved.[6] The traditional view says that when the parent finds fifteen candy wrappers in the child's room, tucked away, it is a message from the child to the parent: "I need nurturing, but I'm not going to allow you to give it to me."

While it is recognized that food issues are impossible to control and may lead to more severe problems later on, traditional professionals recommend other control measures. Parents are told to put locks on their pantries and refrigerators in order to regain control of their homes and to establish authority.[7] Only healthy foods that parents approve of should be in the home. Alarms need to be installed on the door to the child's room to prevent him from leaving the room at night to eat. These measures are recommended in order to put the parent back into control and to create a home where the parent is in charge of providing the food. Thus, the "enemy within" loses his power and control.

A New View

Children with food-related issues generally have trauma related to food in their histories. For a child who hoards, there is a strong likelihood that his

earliest experiences were formed around not having enough food to satisfy his hunger. And more importantly, he may not have had anyone to go
through the step-by-step intimate process of feeding him. The act of feeding
a baby or young child goes far beyond providing for a physical need. Feeding is a time of engagement with the child, a time of bonding with the child,
and a time of providing reassurance and safety for the child. Feeding time
for the baby and young child should be a time of relaxation when parents
are patient with the child, not rushing the child, and being understanding of the child when he turns his head in his easily distracted existence.
It is a time for parents to listen to the child's cues, not forcing the child to
eat more than he needs to eat. This process is a vital time for parents and
children to learn to communicate with one another from an emotional and
intrinsic level.

Many children with trauma experiences did not have these important
interactions in the early years of their lives. The result is that the child has
had negative repetitious conditioning around food. This child has probably
had little or no experience with a secure figure regulating his environment
as it relates to food. This could also mean that the child woke up in the
middle of the night without a parent there to comfort him. The only thing
available was food and the child used the food to find comfort. Thus, when
working with a child with hoarding and/or gorging behaviors, it is important to keep in mind that this child fundamentally had negative experiences
where food was not always available. This child learned that soothing does
not occur through relationships with adults but that soothing occurs in relationship to food. So, there were few, if any, positive experiences when he
could cry and have someone feed him, or there were not enough times when
he had access to enough food with a secure figure to feed him and nurture
him with the food.

It is vital to recognize the impact these experiences have on the child's
developing brain. A part of the brain, called the Supra Chiasmatic Nucleus,
or SCN, sits inside the hypothalamus (the hypothalamus is responsible for
clear thinking, decision making, and regulating the outpouring of stress
from the amygdala). The SCN is a network of thousands of little nerve fibers
that are essentially responsible for the body's circadian rhythms. These circadian responses include the heart rate, blood pressure, digestive responses, body temperature, sleep modulation, and hunger responses. Neglect will
often leave the SCN suppressed due to the body constricting up onto itself,
relying on itself instead of others. Thus, children in this scenario often come
to rely on food for their source of regulation.

Relate the combination of stress and food to your own experiences.
How do you react to food when you are overly stressed? You either overeat

or under-eat. Take this natural reaction and expand upon it with a child with a traumatic history. The child is going to have an exaggerated tendency to either over-eat or under-eat. When it comes to eating, a child with a trauma history may swing from either end of the spectrum on a day-to-day basis. When this child becomes overly stressed, by the end of the day he may shut down and not have eaten anything by dinnertime. Then, when he wakes up in the middle of the night, he gets up and he hoards food. Remember, all behavior arises from a state of stress. Thus, hoarding and gorging occur when a child is in a stress state. This is a child acting out of a fear-based/stressed place.

When the parent finds fifteen candy wrappers in the child's room, tucked away, it is a message from the child to the parent that says: *"My body is craving this candy because I am in a stressful state. My present stressful state shifts me back to a time when I was completely dysregulated, and it is the need for candy that represents my underdeveloped ability to self-soothe."* The child is not eating the candy to make his parents mad, and the child is not intentionally eating the candy as a passive-aggressive way to keep his parents at arm's length. The eating of the candy occurs from an unconscious state. When this child grabs for the candy, his unconscious state is already activated and in full response mode.

> ■
>
> *The child can then begin the process of seeking the parent for regulation, rather than the food.*
>
> ■

The parent should then respond to this act of eating candy in a way that addresses the underlying fear and stress. The parent will want to communicate this understanding to the child from a love-based place. *"Son, I know that when you get stressed out, the first thing you want to do is to go and eat. And, more than anything, you'll want to eat something sweet. Sweet food really helps you calm down."* It is essential that the parent understands and accepts from where this child's behaviors and actions are coming. When the parent can truly see that there is fear underneath this behavior, the parent is then equipped to help the child by responding in love, rather than reacting from fear with the need to address who is in control within the relationship. It is imperative that the child not be judged, chastised, or punished. Otherwise, the child will continue to sneak around behind the parent or at night to satisfy his bodily signals, without including the parent. The parent then communicates a plan of action for the child, offering to help the child when he is stressed out and hungry in the night. *"Son, when you get up in the middle of the night, come and let me know. Wake me up...it's okay. If you wake up and you're scared and stressed out,*

I want to be able to help you."

The child can then begin the process of seeking the parent for regulation, rather than the food. Once the child has come and awakened the parent, the parent should sit with him and lay him back down in bed, helping the child soothe and return to a calm state. If the child still craves a snack, the parent should then understand that this need to eat might take several positive repetitious experiences before it subsides. The parent can then offer to have a snack with the child. It is strongly recommended that the parent actually feed the child, recreating the developmental experiences the child missed. This is not an opportunity for the parent to teach good nutritional habits, though. Sweets are a naturally occurring attachment food. We seek out sweet food when we are stressed. We do not naturally seek out vegetables when we are stressed – only if we are Richard Simmons! Sweet foods initiate the naturally occurring hormones, allowing us to regulate.

In addition to this core intervention, parents are encouraged to do the following:

1. The parent can tell the child a story about neglect. It can be any story that relates to the need for food in order to feel better. This type of story telling will relate to the child's unconscious drives and can be extremely powerful.
2. Throughout the day, the child should have access to plenty of snacks. These snacks should include foods that are naturally sweet: raisins, apples, granola bars, etc. There are many foods on the market that are sweet and fairly nutritious. The refrigerator and the pantry do not need to be locked. Some parents have given their child a "fanny pack" to put around his waist so the food is constantly with him, reassuring him in a tangible way that food will always be available.
3. Begin bottle-feeding your child...yes, begin bottle-feeding your twelve or even fourteen year-old. If a child needs it, regardless of his age, he will take the bottle. The simple gauge is this: if he does not need it, he will not be inclined to take it. Remember that if the child did not receive sufficient developmental nurturing, then he has a barrier in his development. Until the barrier is addressed, the other levels are going to continue to stagger. The bottle-feeding should only occur while the child is in the parent's arms.

When beginning these interventions, it is important to remember that reducing hoarding and gorging behaviors is a systematic process. The parent needs to remain patient. It is easy to revert to traditional shame-based and punitive approaches – the approaches which continue to deny children food and deny children from receiving help at a core level. Many of the traditional approaches actually recreate the neglectful environments that created this behavior initially. With children from orphanages, these old approaches – locking up the kitchen, sending children to their rooms, and demanding that children ask permission to receive food – are essentially recreating the environments of the orphanages from where the behaviors stemmed.

If the child regresses and the parent finds the candy wrappers in the child's room, it is simply a sign that the child was out of his window of tolerance again and that the child was unable to have the awareness or the conscious ability to seek the parent first. It is also a sign that the child continues to fear the parent and continues to lack trust in the parent. It takes time; hence, when regression occurs, the parent needs to continue to stay in a place of love and needs to see this as an opportunity to create more trust and further offer regulation to the child. *"Son, I can tell that you've been really stressed out." "Well, how do you know that, dad?" "I found twenty candy wrappers under your bed, and I know that the only time you hoard food like that is when you're really stressed out, feeling like nobody is really listening to you."* In this example, the parent is able to respond to the child, not react. The parent is able to see the twenty candy wrappers as twenty flashing signals – as a gateway to communicate with the child. It is important to stay focused on the process of change, not the outcome and not the change itself. Slowly and systematically, the child will begin to reduce the need to hoard and gorge.

To continue with the story of the foster mother who found the fifty or more soda cans in her child's room, read how her response was one of mindfulness, understanding, and self-awareness. She writes:

I breathe, reflect, and begin my attempt to relate. With every ounce of me, I attempt to relate as he looks right at me, swears he did not drink that soda and insists that someone else must have put those cans there to set him up. He begins cussing, screaming, and threatening. So, I sit down – way down – on the ground where he is towering over me. I am scared. I don't know what to do in that moment, but I trust in my process, and I reflect on the situation. I realize how disrespected I feel by him. I realize that I am feeling what I think is anger about him not being grateful enough. I decide to put my stuff in a can, put a lid on it and put it away and to go back to relating to him – right then and there. I work really hard to be fully present with him, to be mindful of all that he is and from where he has come. I force myself to picture this huge young man as a crying baby with no one there to meet his needs or to feed him. I ask him, "How much soda do you need to feel fulfilled? Can I take you shopping right now, just you and me, and buy as many cases as you need? You can stack them in your room and you can have them all to yourself." I am trying so hard to be regulated, to be mindful, and to relate to his pain. He stops and, for the first time in the five or more years that I have known him, he sits down with me and tells me the story. The story is of bottles filled with nothing but soda, which he learned to fill by himself by the time he was two years old, while living by himself for days at a time. His mom had a lot of soda as he remembers and that was all he had during these days alone. He told me when he is sad now that he wants soda. I asked him if he had been sad so much of the time with us and he broke my heart (which I put back up on the shelf) when he told me, "Yes."

Parenting Example: Hoarding and Gorging

Scenario: Frankie, a nine year old, is sitting in the therapist's office with his aunt and uncle, with whom he lives. He is sitting on the couch between his aunt and uncle. His aunt begins to complain to the therapist: "Frankie is a thief around food. He doesn't eat much at the table, but afterwards he really puts it away behind our backs. He also stockpiles food like a pack rat in his room, rarely eating it, with most of it rotting in his bedroom."

Traditional View

Frankie is exhibiting several controlling behaviors that need to be addressed. The first immediate issue is that Frankie cannot sit between his aunt and uncle and he will not be allowed to do this at home or in the therapist's office anymore. This positioning of himself is demonstrative of his need to triangulate, divide, and conquer the family members.[8] The therapist then gives the understanding to Frankie's aunt and uncle that food and mealtimes are being used to maintain his control in the home. Because his aunt has expressed on many occasions how important it is for them to have dinner together, Frankie has used this information to purposely disrupt what is important to his aunt – one more attempt at keeping them at arms length. The aunt and uncle are counseled to regain control in the home by implementing control measures, such as locks on the pantry and refrigerator. Frankie is to be allowed in the kitchen only with an adult present. All food is now to be dispersed by the adults[9] and Frankie is to be told and reassured, in a loving manner, that there will be enough for him; he simply needs to ask them politely for it. They are also encouraged to feed sweets to Frankie, only by them and only on their terms. This will promote pleasurable feelings, which will result in a connection to the aunt and uncle.[10]

A New View

Frankie's shift between refusing food to gorging and hoarding food is evidence of trauma around food. The therapist first points out that Frankie has a need to feel safe; hence, he has positioned himself in the room between the two safest people in his life, his aunt and his uncle. His aunt and uncle are encouraged to reassure Frankie in his efforts for safety by softly and tenderly placing an arm around him or placing a hand on his leg. The therapist then addresses the aunt's reactive language when describing Frankie's behavior. In talking, the aunt discloses that while growing up, her father, the primary breadwinner in the home, became terminally ill when she was nine-years old. Her family went from being a middle-class family to receiving food stamps. Food was a commodity in their home and was never wasted. The therapist helps the aunt relate her reaction to Frankie's behaviors to this past experience and helps her to see the correlation in her age at that time and Frankie's current age. The therapist then encourages the aunt and uncle to see Frankie's behavior as a response to stress. His aunt relates her story to Frankie and takes ownership of her reactive stance towards him. She apologizes and encourages Frankie: *"When you feel like stealing food, we want you to come to us. We are not going to punish you anymore. We understand you now. We are here to help you with these feelings. Please let us be here when you're feeling so upset."* A discussion opens up about how hard it is for Frankie to come to the table and eat. Frankie says that he has good memories of his family eating meals together prior to his mother "turning mean" (prior to her alcoholism). He misses his mother and coming to the table reminds him of the happy times with her. Frankie also relates the story about how his mother, after becoming addicted to alcohol, would be unable to get off the couch in order to fix him meals. The aunt and uncle continue to soothe Frankie throughout the session and promise to be open to his erratic eating patterns, in order to help him reduce his food-related responses.

Quick Reference **HOARDING AND GORGING**

Remember that hoarding and gorging:
- Stem from earlier experiences of not having enough food.
- Are an indication that the child did not have an adult to help regulate the food intake.
- Result from negative repetitious experiences around food.
- Happen when the child did not have an adult to nurture and soothe him during the feeding process.
- Result when the circadian rhythms are suppressed.
- Are exaggerated reactive food/stress responses we all naturally have.
- Occur when a child's ability to self-soothe is underdeveloped.

When discovering this behavior, recognize that your child needs you to:
- See this behavior as a sign that he was stressed.
- Approach him with an understanding that is not blame-based or negative.
- Offer to help him when he is feeling overwhelmed and desiring to hoard or gorge food.
- Offer safety through the removal of disciplinary actions.
- Bottle-feed him to revisit an interrupted developmental process.
- Provide him access to snacks throughout his day.
- Remain patient when he regresses.
- Know that he is not doing these behaviors intentionally.

CHAPTER NINE

Aggression

■

"If you are patient in one moment of anger,
you will escape a hundred days of sorrow."
– Chinese Proverb

W e live in an increasingly aggressive society. Anger and aggression are everywhere – on the road, on the big screen, on the news, and yes, at little league games. Children also experience aggression on a daily basis—in the classroom, in the school cafeteria, in the home with siblings, and on the playground.

While many children, especially little boys, go through stages of being aggressive, they typically learn to channel and express the feelings behind this anger in more socially appropriate ways. But when this aggression goes beyond typical childhood behavior, it becomes exceptionally unsettling and extremely uncomfortable for parents and other members of a family. In many cases, it is downright scary. Children with trauma histories often exhibit aggressive behaviors which cannot be compared to other children's behaviors in their intensity, frequency, and duration.

One mother writes:

> It is the violence in my home that I wasn't prepared for. We adopted a cute little boy, two-and-one-half years old, with the most endearing little dimple that lights up his face when he smiles. But when he gets angry, he goes into an uncontrollable rage. It is as if he is possessed. He is violent beyond words. He turns into a wild animal – biting, hitting, kicking, and literally assaulting his family, especially me, his mother. I'm so scared...what is going to happen when he gets older? I'm terrified that he's going to really hurt someone. I never could have believed this kind of violence could be possible from such a small child. It is so unnerving.

Traditional View
The traditional view explains that children with trauma histories thrive on high levels of adrenaline.[1] Therapists point out that these children come from high levels of anger in their prior environments. Not only are these children

accustomed to the anger and turmoil, it is explained that these children are actually comforted by it.[2] The chaos is safe. The fear and instability is what they know best. It is the familiar. They also explain that anger is a way for these children to create externally what is going on internally.[3]

Anger is seen to be a friend to this child – a strong and powerful friend. Whenever the child is feeling weak, sad, or any other emotion that is painful to him, the child can call upon his anger to take control of the situation. He knows that people respond to anger by getting angry back. The child is then able to control the emotional states of the people around him.[4] Anger puts the other person (usually the parent) in a defensive mode – away from a place of love and nurturing. The traditional explanation further explains that this anger then creates emotional safety for the child, providing a wall of security to guard against vulnerability – yet another tool to keep the parents at arm's length.[5]

One of the most popular parenting techniques recommended for parents is to use a paradoxical approach with a child who typically becomes angry and aggressive.[6][7][8] This keeps the parent in control and keeps the parent from being taken hostage to the child's aggressive state, keeping the child from "winning" within the parent-child relationship. A classic example would be for a parent to tell his eight year-old child to turn off the television because it is dinnertime and that he may go ahead and have a tantrum. This double bind is necessary in order for the child to know that the parent is strong, per-sistent, and definitely in charge.[9] If the child has a tantrum, the child is doing what the parent instructed him to do. If the child refuses to have a tantrum, the parent wins because a tantrum has been avoided. Parents are told to pre-dict the child's behavior in order for the parent to stay in charge, which then allows the child to find a way out of his negative patterned behaviors.[10]

A New View
Three foundational principles need to be understood to truly see what creates a child who looks "possessed" or acts like a "wild animal," as described by the mother at the beginning of this chapter. First, a child's aggressive behaviors arise from a state of stress. This stress is induced by the presence of fear. Second, this fear state presents itself as a mask of anger. We often become so threatened by the anger that we fail to understand that this feeling of anger originates and is driven from fear. And third, a child does not consciously act in an angry/fearful state. A child is not consciously driven to aggression in order to create disruption in relationships. Trauma impacts a child's state level of memory, causing him to behave aggressively when in a state of stress or fear.

The true understanding of an aggressive child is found in brain research.

Research shows that a child's neurophysiological system is impacted by trauma; the amygdala becomes hypersensitive to threat. The over-sensitized amygdala becomes reactive based on stimulation through the child's sensory pathways, primarily through the sense of smell, vision, body language, temperature, and touch. Thus, when a child is prone to a hyperaroused state, he is literally hard-wired to go into a "super-charged" mode. Although initially starting out in a frozen state, within a millisecond, the child enters into a reactive state of fight; aggressive and defensive behaviors are then demonstrated. The child is not aggressive out of spite, meanness, or out of hate. Rather, the child is aggressive out of a survival state. The child is, in many instances, in a place of absolute terror.

The only time we seek to change someone else's behavior is when we ourselves feel threatened or scared.

As mom walks towards the child, the child's perception, in his hyperaroused state, becomes distorted and the child becomes overwhelmed in his thinking process. His mother, who two seconds ago was the apple of his eye, has now become a monster ready to attack him, or even kill him. So, the child, in his distorted fear state, attacks his mother, biting her, kicking her, spitting on her, and hitting her.

To add to this, the parent's immediate reaction to the child is that the child is not safe. The child has now become a threat to the parent. Yes, the cute little toddler with the adorable dimple has now become a threat within his very own home. In many cases, the state level memory quickly becomes activated within the parent, awakening the traumatic stress that the parent experienced in the past. In this condition, the parent's ability to be flexible and to determine what is truly a threat, to see the child's fear, and to remain calm is greatly diminished.

A parent's automatic reaction is to control this child in an attempt to secure the environment. It is important to note that the only time we seek to control is when we are in a fear state. The only time we seek to change someone else's behavior is when we ourselves feel threatened or scared. Thus, it is the parent's own fear state that is driving the controlling parental behaviors. The combination of the parent's fear state and the child's fear state then creates an environment filled with hate, chaos, and violence.

Aggression from a child of any age can be scary for a parent. But as little children become young adults, growing taller and stronger than their parents, it becomes terrifying for parents. Let us look at three scenarios of aggressive behaviors from three different developmental stages. These examples will show how a parent can respond to these behaviors in order to keep the scenarios from intensifying and igniting.

Scenario 1: Tina is a three year-old toddler who was removed from her biological mother at the age of nine months. Her biological mother was the victim of severe domestic violence throughout her pregnancy with Tina. Now at three, other parents secretly refer to Tina as "the terrorist of the play-ground." She typically hits other children for no apparent reason, throws sand in their faces, and pushes them off the swings. Today, Tina is playing in the park with four other children. After thirty-minutes of play, Tina's regulatory system has become taxed and she has moved into a state of dysregulation, unbeknownst to her foster mother. Suddenly, one of the children playing with Tina bumps into Tina. BOOM! Tina starts pushing and hitting the child. As Tina attacks, her aggression becomes more and more intense; her aggression escalates as the other child begins to fight back with Tina. Within a matter of seconds, Tina went from what looked like a calm state to an aggressive and hostile state.

Our first reaction would be to pull Tina out, put her in time-out for her behavior, and tell her that hitting is not nice. Yet, we have to begin to see these types of situations differently if we are to help Tina's regulatory system develop appropriately. Recognizing first that peer interaction is a stress-inducing event, we can then see that Tina was beyond her stress tolerance. Her regulatory system was activated and ready to discharge the build up of energy at any moment. It would have been prudent of Tina's foster mother to recognize that thirty minutes of play was too much for Tina, pulling Tina in with her for a "Time-In" prior to the incident. Tina could have sat with her foster mother for a few minutes, which would then have allowed Tina to shift back into a calm state, ready to return to safely playing with the other children.

In cases such as this where it was too late and Tina already became aggressive, her foster mother could help Tina understand that she was too stressed to play at that moment. Her foster mother could say, "Tina, you look so scared right now. Come sit with me, sweetheart. You're okay...nobody is going to hurt you. I'm going to keep you safe. " Tina's foster mother would then be addressing Tina at her state level of survival, calming her activated primal fear stored within the cells of Tina's body. Tina's foster mother would then have become Tina's external hippocampus, allowing the body system to regulate and return to a state of calm. Later in the day, when both Tina and her foster mother are calm, the life lesson of teaching Tina that hitting is wrong could take place. Tina would more easily absorb this moral teaching when her body system is calm and regulated.

Scenario 2: Let us revisit the example given earlier when describing the traditional attachment parenting approach with the eight year old who was instructed to turn off the television. Mom says, "It's time to eat dinner; please turn off the TV, Sam." Sam, in turn, throws the remote control and yells, "I hate you!" This type of immediate, explosive reaction indicates that Sam does not feel safe most of the time within his own home. He is living in a hyper-vigilant state and it only takes one simple directive from the parent for him to have a complete emotional meltdown. If mom were to react to Sam in a controlling manner, the chances are high that the situation would escalate into hitting, kicking, and yelling behaviors, as has been the pattern in the years previous.

Instead, mom has to recognize that Sam lives in a continual state of fear and in a continual state of alert, ready at a moment's notice to attack. In this understanding, mom goes to Sam ten minutes before it is time to eat dinner. She sits down on the couch with him, puts her arm around him to physically engage him, and gently says, "Honey, in about five minutes we are going to have to turn off the TV. Okay?" No answer is necessary and mom should not expect an answer at this point. Sam, then, is given time to process the directive on his own.

Mom comes back five minutes later and says, "Honey, it is time to turn the TV off. I know you get really scared when it is time to turn off the TV because you are afraid we will never turn it back on again (that is Sam's reality because stress causes confused and distorted thinking). When you get scared like this, you usually get really mad. Actually, you look really mad right now. I want you to tell me you're mad. Really, tell me you're angry you have to turn the TV off." Mom is giving Sam permission to be angry because that is the only way he has known up to this point in his development to express himself. She is not telling him to get angry as a double bind as described earlier. She really wants to absorb his anger for him. She says it with passion, "Tell me you're angry, son. I want to know how mad it makes you." Mom is meeting Sam in his emotional place and giving him the space and safety to work through his dysregulation. When

■

Aggressive children are seeking regulation and expressing this deep-seated need through their behaviors.

■

he says, "Yeah, I'm mad" with little affect, she says, "Yes, you're mad. Tell me again louder, with more feeling, 'I'm mad.'" Mom is helping Sam express himself verbally in order to help him discharge the build up of energy within his body system.

Scenario 3: Joshua is a 14 year-old child whose behavior has been increasing in its level of violence, especially since turning 13 a year ago. To date, Joshua's parents have managed to restrain him during his violent rages in order to prevent serious injury. Joshua walks in the door after school, slams the door, throws his backpack on the floor, and flings his shoes off on the way to his room. Dad interrupts this daily pilgrimage to his room by calmly saying, "Joshua, how was your day?" Joshua, in his dysregulated state replies, "It sucked. What's it to you anyway?" Dad immediately shifts into a controlling mode, stands up to show his physical stature, deepens his voice, and says, "You're not going to talk to me that way. Get over here, son!" Joshua quickly turns around, increases his stride towards his father, puts out his hands to aggressively push his father, and says, "I'll talk to you any damn way I please."

Dad has officially been triggered into a fear state. In order to relate to Joshua, though, dad has to first see that his own fear has been triggered. Dad has to realize when Joshua is in a state of arousal that the most effective way to help Joshua is to come down from his own arousal state and to understand where Joshua is emotionally. In this understanding, dad can then maintain his own regulation. It has been shown that the calmer amygdala has the ability to soothe the less regulated amygdala.

So, instead, after dad hears Joshua's initial disrespectful response, dad takes a few deep breaths, which allow him to stay regulated and to stay in touch with Joshua's emotional state. Dad then follows Joshua into his room and sits on the bed without saying a word. Words do not have to be communicated at this point. The essence is to create a relationship that will allow regulation to seep in without pouring fuel on the flame of dysregulation and aggression. Then, after a few minutes, dad says, "Son, I see you had a tough day today." Joshua continues with the belligerent language and says, "You're damn right! I hate my fucking school and my teachers are assholes." Dad says, "Wow. I remember middle school. I remember how rough it was. What happened today, son?" Dad is relating through communication and he is meeting Joshua in Joshua's dysregulated state. Dad keeps processing with Joshua and after awhile, gets up, walks to the doorway, and says, "Joshua, I'll be in my office; come let me know if you need me for anything."

Later that night, dad comes to Joshua, sits down and says, "Josh, this afternoon you were really nasty to me when you got home. I know you were upset, but that kind of language upsets me and I feel quite disrespected when you talk to me that way. How about next time you just say, 'I had a bad day, Dad'?" This communication regarding Joshua's unacceptable language occurs in a calm state, where Joshua is open to listening and open to making a commitment to do better next time. Dad was able to diffuse a potentially aggressive scene simply by understanding and relating to Joshua – meeting Joshua in his place of hyper-arousal.

Parents need to see anger as fear. This fear-dynamic can then be used in order to provide an environment conducive to not only change, but to healing. Aggressive children are seeking regulation and expressing this deep-seated need through their behaviors. They need to be given the emotional space in order to work through their dysregulation. In many cases, while seeking regulation, they are actually unable to receive it from the parent, which typically gets the parent frustrated and triggered back into a fearful state. The parent needs to physically step back in order to reduce the threat and to allow the child the space he needs in order for the upper level thinking to become active. Parents need to realize that the aggression is not directed at them personally; it is aggression towards survival. Lastly, parents have to see their own fear reaction and be in touch with their own fears in order to respond to their child from a place of love, instead of reacting to their child from a state of fear (see Chapter 5).

Parenting Example: Aggression

Scenario: Tommy is an adopted 16 year old with a history of rageful, aggressive, and threatening behaviors in the home. Since the age of twelve, he has become increasingly abusive and violent, threatening to hurt family members. Now he regularly works out in the gym and has become physically stronger. All attempts at having him placed in an inpatient program for anger management have failed. Suddenly one night, he gets into an argument with his older brother, flies into a rage, and breaks his brother's nose.

Traditional View

Tommy is effectively holding this family hostage by his uncontrollable anger outbursts and combative behaviors. We have to realistically see that Tommy is demonstrating behaviors that are only warnings of things to come, perhaps even murdering somebody in the future. Punishing him only ignites his rages. He is refusing to go to therapy, so finding a counselor really is not an option. At this point, the family has only a few options in order to provide safety for the other family members. They can call the police and have Tommy arrested. They can continue to attempt to manage Tommy at home by taking a couple of proactive steps. The parents can sleep in shifts to ensure family safety from this child (which is actually a good idea for Tommy to know that someone is watching him all the time). The family, excluding Tommy, can take a self-defense course. Tommy should not be included in this self-defense course because that would be akin to giving Tommy another weapon to use against the family. Additionally, they can ask Tommy to leave the home, or they can ultimately turn Tommy over to the county foster care system. [11]

New View

The first step for this family is to realize the intense fear that has permeated into every interaction with every family member on a day-to-day basis. Family members are living out of the fear from the past, fearing and avoiding the present, and most certainly living in fear of the future. The parents need to realize that Tommy has been acting out aggressively from a primal state of fear, not anger. When they are able to see Tommy as a scared child, instead of an angry child, they will be able to relate to him and to help him get in touch with the fear driving his behaviors. The parents need to realize that early trauma has impacted Tommy's state level of memory and that Tommy is acting out of a survival mode. Tommy's regulatory system is insufficient to be around his older brother without an adult nearby to help regulate the interaction. The next time Tommy begins to shift into his aggressive state and yell aggressive threats, his parent needs to say to him, "Tommy, you must be really scared right now. By you telling me that you're going to kill me, that only means that you're really scared that someone might kill you." The parent then closes the door of the room, creating physical containment for Tommy, and the parent sits on the floor, lessening the perceived threat of the parent. After taking some deep breaths and getting in touch with his own fear, the parent then invites Tommy to express his emotions, "Tommy, tell me how scared you are right now. I'm not going anywhere...I'm right here with you. You're not in trouble and I'm not sending you away." The parent waits patiently for Tommy's next cue. The parent continues to stay with Tommy, not trying to force, change, or control Tommy. The parent continues to invite and relate to Tommy from a safe, non-threatening, love based place. Tommy will ultimately, even if it takes three or four hours – or even six hours – be able to safely discharge some of the bound up, fear-driven energy within his body.

Quick Reference   **AGGRESSION**

Remember that aggression:
- Arises from a state of stress.
- Is a fear-based behavior.
- Is not a conscious act to create chaos or harm.
- Occurs when the brain's amygdala becomes hyper-sensitive to threat.
- Easily puts the parent in a state of fear.
- Is a sign of a scared child, not an angry child.
- Is an act towards survival and is not directed at the parent.

When experiencing this behavior, recognize that your child needs you to:
- Relate to the fear within yourself that is triggered by the aggression.
- Understand that he is simply seeking regulation.
- Stay regulated in order to help in regulating him.
- Understand that he is not trying to create chaos because chaos really does not feel good.
- Pull him in for a "Time-In."
- Be aware that the only time we seek to control is when we are scared, so stay flexible.
- He is not pushing you away and, in fact, needs you more than ever during the aggressive behavior.

CHAPTER TEN

Defiance

■

"A man's ethical behavior should be based effectually on sympathy, education, and social ties; no religious basis is necessary. Man would indeed be in a poor way if he had to be restrained by fear of punishment and hope of reward after death."

– Albert Einstein

While every child has "ornery" moments, a child classified as defiant is a child who takes being ornery to the extraordinary. It is a child who takes autonomy to the extreme. Just like the skateboarder who simply uses his skateboard to skate down the sidewalk, and then switches to the extreme by flying off an eight-foot ledge and landing on a two-inch metal handrail. An attachment-challenged child is often seen to take defiance to this intensity. These children are often described as being extremely disobedient, exceedingly rebellious, overly insolent, and completely non-cooperative. They can demonstrate a refusal to being controlled by anybody and constantly test limits. Defiance is one of the classic symptoms on a child attachment checklist, usually being described as "oppositional, argumentative, defiant" and as a child with "extreme control problems."

The typical prognosis by professionals for children and adolescents who do not work out their defiant behavior in their youth is often grim, at best. Professionals in the field of mental health often tell parents that disruptive behavior disorders can lead to a lifetime of problems. The problems they list include social dysfunction, anti-social behavior, and poor adjustment. They further expand on this by explaining that not only will these children suffer within themselves, but their families, peers, and society as a whole will suffer.

Parents seeking help for dealing with their defiant child often find themselves in a more severe situation after following the advice of professionals. A mother describes her situation:

> We sought help for Joseph, our five year old, who was exceptionally defiant to even the simplest of requests. We sought the counsel of a behavioral analyst and used the intervention of 'Extinction.' We used this method when Joseph would refuse a request. We were instructed to stay focused only on the instruction given until Joseph conformed. He became completely oppositional and

outraged with this intervention. At times, it would take Joseph up to three hours to follow a simple instruction such as putting on his shoes when it was time to go to the store. His response using this method switched from being just defiant to aggressive. It was so severe that he smashed a window with his bare hands, charged me with a pair of scissors, and threw heavy objects at me, intending to hurt me. It is disheartening and frightening to be following the advice of a well-known professional and to see our home become so out-of control.

Traditional View

Traditional professionals explain that the defiant behaviors from attachment- challenged children are an outward expression of the child's internal intolerance of having other people's limits placed upon them. These children are seen to be constantly testing, baiting, and pushing limits in an attempt to see what kind of a reaction they will receive from the adult in charge. Thus, parents are told that their child is in a constant battle for control of the environment.[1] Parents are given strict counseling to stay in control and to especially stay in control of their own emotions.[2] If the child manages to upset the parent, this puts the child back into control. In this view, it is crucial that parental anger be avoided.[3] Emphasis is placed on the perception that the child must do what is asked by the parent in order for an appropriate parent-child relationship to develop.[4]

The defiant behaviors in these children can be either outright refusals to comply by choice[5] or more covert in nature.[6] Traditionally the child who complies readily with a parental instruction, yet "mistakenly forgets" or does not properly complete the task, is seen as manipulative and passive-aggressive. Thus, even when appearing to comply, the child is actually non-compliant – always "off by a hair."[7] When Jenny is asked to put the dishes in the dishwasher and "inadvertently" leaves one spoon in the sink, she is giving a message to her parents that she is doing what they have asked, but that she is not really doing what they have asked. Thus, Jenny is seen in the traditional model as passive-aggressive, maintaining control, and keeping her parents on the peripheral.[8]

One traditional approach is to have children complete their chores "fast and snappy, right the first time, Mom and Dad's way."[9] If the child fails to comply in this manner, the response from the parent is to make a statement to the child that will make the child "think" in order to avoid control battles and to have the child become insightful. So when Jimmy is asked to mow the lawn prior to eating dinner and refuses or losses track of time, Mom can say to him, "Son, you are free to join your family for your next meal as long as the lawn is mowed." The idea of this approach is that Jimmy then learns that there are choices in the "real world" and that he will have the opportunity to make the right choice next time.[10]

New View

As humans, we are a reactive species. When we experience an event that is unfamiliar to us, we will perceive that event as a threat until deemed otherwise. Our immediate reaction will almost always be that of a freeze reaction; we then determine whether to fight or flee – whether to enter into a hyper-aroused state or a hypo-aroused state. When applying this understanding to an oppositional-defiant child, it can be seen that the child is fundamentally a hypo-aroused child. A defiant child is essentially a scared child. A child in this hypo-aroused state, or shutdown state, has the potential for then moving swiftly into a hyper-aroused state, or aggressive state.

Reflect on the example of Joseph, the five-year-old defiant child who was being forced through a behavioral technique to follow his parent's directive. His mother described the situation as turning from defiance to aggression. While Joseph's initial fear manifested itself into refusing behavior, this fear state was then fed with more fear by his mother's reaction, quickly shifting Joseph into an aggressive, hyper-aroused state.

> ■
> *A defiant child is essentially a scared child.*
> ■

For children with trauma histories, it can be *any* request from the parent that creates a feeling of threat. A parental request at any level (yes, simply being asked to take out the trash or simply to put on his shoes) can be one that shifts the child into a fear state due to perceiving the directive as a threat. Dependent on the history, this child may be actually terrified. In that moment, the child cannot determine whether the parent's request is safe or not. He immediately goes into freeze mode, and then becomes defiant to the parent's request. In that moment, the child has to be defiant. There is no other alternative.

The essence of defiance is fear. A child needs to be given emotional space and in many cases, physical space, to perceive that the request is not a threat. This is a traumatic stress issue. It is not an issue of the child working to control or manipulate the parent. It is not an issue of the child testing the limits or baiting the parent to see how he can make his parent become emotionally reactive. Defiance is a fundamental issue of feeling threatened and overwhelmed with fear.

After parents give a request, they need to step back and give the child space to process the fear. Giving children emotional space helps them to soothe and process their fear state, allowing them then to rationally interpret the request as safe. This is only effective if the parent is truly calm. Parents have to recognize and acknowledge their own internal reactions to their child's defiant behaviors. Perhaps it is a reaction of feeling powerless, a feeling of being disrespected, or a feeling of fear of the child not developing an attachment to the parent. The parent needs to work to stay in a calm state in order to help the child then feel safe. Remember, the calmer amgydala has the ability to soothe the aroused amgydala.

There are several predictable areas of defiance for children with trauma histories. Some of these include transition, school-time, bath-time, bedtime, and homework. Let us take a look at each one of these particular areas with parenting examples to show how to help the child's fear state be reduced and eventually eliminated.

Transition: Adopted children and children in foster care often demonstrate defiance around the issue of transition. These children need us to recognize that transitional stress is the result of early childhood experiences. For the newborn adopted at birth, the very first transition was being placed from the arms of his birth mother to the arms of his adoptive mother. For the two-year old, it happened when the caseworker arrived at the biological home and the child was driven away, never to return home again. For the eight year old who was removed from the orphanage by his adoptive parents after living in the same orphanage since birth, transitional trauma occurred amongst strangers who communicated in a different language. These are all examples of trauma around transition.

They are not equipped to soothe the overload of stress that floods their body-mind systems at nighttime.

The result is that these children in the above examples can have a negative association with any type of transition in the future. The child needs the parent to recognize and acknowledge that this is the fundamental dynamic behind the defiance.

Reflecting back on Joseph, the five-year old, Mom could address this by saying, "Joseph, honey, can you please put your shoes on? We need to go to the store." Joseph sits down on the floor, crosses his arms and says, "No." Mom needs to reflect on the origin of this defiance and defensive posture. Recognizing that he indeed has early trauma around transition, Mom sits down on the floor, puts her arm around Joseph and says, "It must be really scary to leave our home, even to go to the store. It is going to be okay, honey. I am not going to let anything separate us when we are gone. I love you and we will be coming right back home."

School-time: Many children, while not being out-right defiant like Joseph, demonstrate avoiding behaviors, or what appear to be more passive aggressive behaviors. Julie, a twelve-year old, constantly cannot get ready on time for school. Her mother is at her breaking edge seeing Julie "paddycak-ing" around in the morning instead of being focused on the morning tasks at hand. Julie needs her mother to recognize that this "putzing" behavior is a reflection of the fear that is ignited every morning when even thinking about going to school. In Julie's case, she was taken from school because of abuse in her home, never to return home to be with her biological mother again. Thus, Julie revisits the fear of going to school and never coming home every morn-ing when thinking about getting on her school bus. Giving consequences for this behavior, telling Julie she needs to make better choices in the morning, or taking away privileges will not address the sheer terror driving her behav-ior.

Bath-time: Children's case files throughout the United States are filled with stories of abuse that occurred in the bathroom of the child's home. In the case of international adoptions, children have related horror stories of being forced to take cold showers while living in the orphanage. Thus, defiance around bath-time routine is exceptionally common. Defiance at bath-time is trauma induced. Addressing this behavior through smell-good charts, placing the child in a different room (such as the laundry room) to eat, or any other technique designed to have the child make a better choice at bath-time[11] disre-gards the unthinkable trauma that occurred in the child's past.

After five years of battling it out with her daughter at bath-time, a mother relates the story of why bath-time was such a defiant time.

> Once I was able to accept her struggle with taking a shower, I calmly offered to be with her in the bathroom and to be pres-ent with her in case she needed me. After taking the first shower without a tantrum in five long years, my daughter was finally able to share this with me: 'Mom, the guy who sexually molested me used to make me take a shower with him.

Bedtime: Bedtime fears for traumatized children go far beyond the "Boo-gie Man" in the closet. Again, nighttime trauma experiences are pervasive for adopted and foster care children. Very real fears stem from nights of being sexually abused by fathers or uncles living in the home. Very real fears stem from being terrified of making a single noise in the orphanage with twenty-five other children as the orphanage worker stood guard. Very real fears stem from being removed from home in the middle of the night by a caseworker due to abuse allegations. Children need their parents to acknowledge and rec-ognize these nighttime fears. They are not equipped to soothe the overload of stress that floods their body-mind systems at nighttime. Bedtime hassles are signs of stress overload, not of manipulation or defiance. Giving a child extra chores or a consequence for not adhering to a strict bed time[12] misses the opportunity for the parent to soothe and help the child in his healing process.

A father writes:

Every night, night after night, my daughter would fiddle-faddle around at bedtime. She'd say she needed a drink of water. She'd aimlessly walk around the house. She'd always need one more thing from me. Then, when she did go to bed, she would always leave the hall light on. I had asked her at least fifty times to turn that light off. I was at my wits end until I realized that this behavior was simply a communication of something deeper. When I finally sat with her one night, calm and open to her process, I asked her what made it so difficult to go to bed at night. She said, 'I don't like the dark, daddy. It scares me that when I wake up in the morning you won't be here. I'm so scared you'll be dead.' Then I reflected on how her mother died three years ago from a brain hemorrhage in the middle of the night.

<u>Homework</u>: Children with trauma histories often have immediate reactions to even the thought of doing homework. Parents need to recognize this as fear – not as defiance – in order to stop the cycle of negative repetitious conditioning. Forcing the child to sit and do his homework by giving him a choice of finishing the homework and then having playtime or making him sit until he decides he is "ready" is unproductive and creates more fear in the child for the next day. Saying that homework is 100 percent the child's responsibility and having the attitude that each school grade is available to the child for as many times as needed[13] does not address the child's inability to self-soothe when faced with fear.

Daniel Goleman, in his book *Emotional Intelligence*, explains that "students who are anxious, angry, or depressed don't learn; people who are caught in these states do not take in information efficiently or deal with it well."[14] So instead of pushing the child and forcing learning to happen, thereby creating negative repetitious conditioning and more fear, the parent's new understanding is that the child simply cannot learn in this emotional state. The new view allows the parent to work to attend to the unconscious fear by saying, "I know that it really scares you to think about doing your homework. Everyday when it is time to do homework, you look like you're in a total panic, sweetheart." The parent's responsibility is to help shift the child out of the state of fear by talking to the child and working to uncover the fear that is driving these resistant behaviors. Perhaps it is the expectation of being perfect in order to be loved instead of being abandoned, as in the past. The child's unconscious is saying, "If I'm perfect, then I'm lovable. If I'm lovable, then I'm safe. If I'm safe, then I won't be hurt anymore. I've got to be perfect." This type of unconscious thought becomes so overwhelming and produces so much stress that the cognitive brain is unable to think logically. The child becomes so overwhelmed with the need to be perfect that the thinking brain literally becomes inaccessible. So, the parent says, "I love you and I'm here forever for you. Your homework does not determine your place in this family. Tell me how scary homework is for you."

Parenting Example: Defiance

Scenario: Peter is a 14 year old who was hospitalized just last week for violently acting out and threatening to kill his younger brother. Dad comes home after an evening out to find chocolate syrup on the counter top and on the floor. He walks in and sees Peter watching TV and eating an ice cream sundae. Dad asks Peter to clean up his mess in the kitchen and Peter responds, "Man, I'm busy watching my show. You're always picking on me."

Traditional View

Dad remembers that his therapist has stressed the importance of the child being respectful to the parent at all times, especially after being allowed back into the home from the hospital. Peter is clearly being disrespectful to his father. Dad also remembers that his goal as Peter's parent is not to stop his child's behavior in so much as it is to lower the negative impact on the parents' lives.[15] Thus, the best approach to such a disrespectful response from Peter would be to simply remove the one who is impacting the family negatively – Peter. Dad has an "on-call" respite caretaker, whom he then calls to pickup Peter immediately. When the respite worker arrives at the home twenty minutes later, Dad calmly and matter-of-factly tells Peter he will be going with Ms. Jane. Peter is given no explanation, and Dad knows he does not need to defend his parenting decision.[16] Peter leaves the home for two days and, when asked if he would like to return home, it is made clear that Peter will need to respect his father in order to be part of the family. This follows the basic belief of the traditional approach that being a part of a family makes a child feel good. Thus, the next time Peter is given a parental directive, he will be more inclined to make the right choice and respectfully respond to the directive.

A New View

First, Dad realizes that a fourteen year old who leaves syrup on the counter top and on the floor is not really a fourteen year old, but more of a five year old. Second, Dad takes a deep breath and considers his own stress that he is bringing into the interaction with his son (stress from work, stress from having to pay for the hospital stay, etc.). Third, Dad realizes that Peter was recently released from the hospital and is certainly hypersensitive to the threat of being returned to the hospital. Dad takes a few deep breaths, processes the dynamics listed above, and walks into the living room again. Dad puts his arm around Peter this time and says, "When you're through with your show, could you please come in the kitchen and clean up?" Dad gives Peter a loving one-armed hug and walks away from Peter. (Dad is giving Peter the physical and emotional space he needs to determine that Dad's request is safe and is not a threat.) At the first commercial, Peter gets up and walks into the kitchen, cleans up his mess, and goes back to finish his show. Dad thanks Peter for cleaning up and they both go to bed peacefully. The next morning, Dad and Peter are sitting at the kitchen table having breakfast. Dad senses that Peter is calm, so Dad initiates a conversation regarding Peter's first response the previous night. Dad says, "Peter, last night when I walked in and found the syrup all over the kitchen, it was frustrating for me. Then, when I asked you to clean it up, you were quite reactive to me. I know that it was scary going to that hospital last week, and you're scared you'll have to go back again, but I'd appreciate it if you could be more respectful to me. Okay, Son?" Peter lowers his head in shame for being disrespectful, and says, "Okay, Dad." Dad reassures Peter he is not going back to the hospital and reconnects with his son physically and emotionally to give him safety and comfort.

Quick Reference **DEFIANCE**

Remember that defiance:
- Is grounded in fear – it is a fear reaction.
- Is preceded by a freeze response.
- Can move quickly to aggression if fed with more fear.
- Happens when a child perceives a request as a threat, even the simplest of requests.
- Is predictable in four areas for children with trauma histories:
  - transition
  - school-time
  - bath-time
  - bedtime

When discovering this behavior, recognize that your child needs you to:
- First be aware of your own reaction to the defiance.
- Step back and give him space to process the fear.
- Verbally acknowledge the fear to him in a loving way.
- Listen to the defiance and reflect upon this unconscious response.
- Link this defiance to his past experiences.
- Validate the trauma feeding the defiant fear-based reaction.
- Interrupt any negative repetitious conditioning.
- Understand that he cannot make logical choices in this fear state.
- Open up communication in order to express this fear with you.
- Teach the life lesson later when he is calm and more cognizant.

CHAPTER ELEVEN
Lack of Eye Contact

∎

"You can close your eyes to reality but not to memories."
– Stanislaw Lec, Polish writer

From a very young age, we are taught to look another person in the eyes when being spoken to or when speaking. Communication experts teach us to make strong eye contact if we desire connection. The American culture interprets lack of eye contact as showing a lack of interest and being disrespectful.

Beyond this, the eyes are often said to be the windows to the soul. Francis Johnson, an English theologian, is quoted as saying, "The balls of sight are so formed, that one man's eyes are spectacles to another, to read his heart from within." This idea of connecting to one's heart through the eyes has also been at the forefront of attachment therapy. Traditionally, eye contact, or lack of eye contact, has been a principle behavior when referring to children with reactive attachment disorder. The eyes have been seen to be a direct measurement of a child's attachment and of his ability to give and receive love.

Traditional View

The traditional view believes that eye contact is a crucial component of determining whether a child has a secure attachment.[1] It proposes that children with reactive attachment disorder are unable to use eye contact for connection and that they cannot use eye contact for closeness or positive communication.[2] Additionally, the traditional view interprets that when a child does use eye contact, it is for negative reasons, such as to manipulate or to dominate. Traditional sources state that the *only* time attachment challenged children are able to make eye contact is when they are lying,[3] extremely angry,[4] or controlling. Children are described as using their eyes to seduce or threaten caregivers[5] in an effort to disarm them. Eye contact is also described to be skillfully used by these children to charm strangers.[6]

Traditional attachment therapists use eye contact in sessions as a principal tool for creating attachment. Eye contact is seen as one of the first tasks to be accomplished before significant therapy can be accomplished, and therapists insist on nearly constant eye contact during sessions.[7] Attachment-challenged children are expected to maintain this eye contact in order to submit their control to either the therapist or the parent. It is explained that these children will consistently avoid eye contact whenever they do not feel in control of the situation,[8] thus it is imperative that they use eye contact in order to form trusting relationships, especially within the therapeutic environment. During other therapeutic techniques where the parent is holding the child, the parent is often instructed to insist and fight for complete eye contact, even at the extent of physically forcing the child to look at the parent.[9] Parenting experts recommend that every communication with the child be made with the child looking directly at the parent.[10]

New View

When it comes to understanding a child's inability to make strong eye contact, a review of Principle #1 (*All negative behavior arises from an unconscious, fear-based state*) needs to be conducted. According to this principle, a child who lacks the ability to make eye contact is a child in a state of fear. It is about a child who is scared – a child who is being driven from an unconscious place by fear.

The traditional view of the lack of eye contact, discussed previously, interprets this behavior from a negative posture. This view says that if a child is not making eye contact, then he is not listening, he is not really connecting with the parent or caregiver, and he is trying to stay in charge. These are all fear-based reasons that scare parents when their children exhibit this behavior. These interpretations, in and of themselves, create barriers in the parent-child relationship.

The new view, with a love-based foundation, offers a gentler explanation, backed by neurological research. From brain research, it is understood that contact with the human eye is the most direct way to stimulate the frontal lobe of the brain. This part of the brain is called the orbital frontal cortex (OFC). The OFC is considered to be the executive control center for a human's social and emotional functioning. Eye contact is the most direct way to stimulate this area. The OFC and the hippocampus both have a direct responsibility for calming the body's stress response system. Thus, when the OFC and hippocampus are being overwhelmed by stress, it requires an enormous amount of energy for the body to regulate at that Moment. Considering that the eyes are sensory pathways, it needs to be acknowledged that the use of the eyes creates more stimulation. Thus, looking at the parent with direct eye contact in this moment of stress becomes overwhelming. In fact, it is one of the most overwhelming directives a parent could ask a child to do when the child is in a state of stress.

In order to understand fully this principle and relate to this explanation, you will need to see it in yourself in order for you to see it clearly in your child. The next time you are really stressed or have slipped into a high arousal state, be mindful of your response – notice how little you make eye contact. Many times we not only look away from those around us, we also shrug off their physical touch. We cut off the stimulation to our sensory pathways because it is simply too much for us to process.

Eye contact is one of the first responses to cease in the midst of stress for anyone, especially traumatized children. Traumatized children are extremely sensitive to threats in the environment, which trigger their stress reactions. These triggers, or "associational connections," easily lead traumatized children into an emotional state of fear, which, in turn, dictates their behavior. So what is seen is a child who diverts his gaze and ceases to make eye contact. The child is not purposely avoiding eye contact to control the parent, nor is he maintaining his sense of control by selectively not listening to the parent. The child does not want to look at the parent because any more eye stimulation may drive him out of his body-mind system. Any more may literally make him feel as if his head is going to pop off!

When a child looks away from the parent, the parent needs to "listen" to this behavior from a modality of love, backed by a neurological understanding. The child is saying, "I can't take anymore stimulation! If I keep looking at you, it will be way too much."

Our body-mind can only take in a limited amount of stimulation. Deepak Chopra, M.D. explains that our body-mind system can only take in a billionth of the amount of sensory information around us at any given time. Relate this to yourself at this Moment. Are you presently aware of the temperature of the room, the way your clothes sit on your body, the texture of the book you are holding, the noises in the room, the noises coming from outside, the taste in your mouth, the smell of your environment, the muscle tightness in your shoulder or leg? We are incapable of creating an alert awareness of all this at one time while staying engaged and focused on our task at hand. We would go crazy if we had to stay alert to every stimulus within both our internal beings and our external environment.

What prevents us from becoming over-stimulated is our regulatory systems. A well-developed regulatory system is equipped to keep the body-mind from becoming overwhelmed; it modulates, it regulates, it calls upon specific senses when appropriate in a balanced and regulated way. The human body will automatically filter out those stimuli that it deems unnecessary to be at the forefront of our consciousness. It is an ever-changing, ever-balancing system at work to keep us in a balanced and regulated state. Most adults have a well-developed regulatory system that is intact and is able to shift from Moments of overwhelm back to a state of balance, all within a millisecond. These experiences of shifting from a state of balance to a state of overwhelm happen countless times throughout the day. However, traumatized children do not have this regulatory flexibility. It is impossible for their systems. Thus, when it comes to making eye contact when they are stressed, it is not a matter of "making a choice" or "giving over the control" to the parent.

The traditional view for the attachment-challenged child says, "He has to make eye contact with you. Tell him to look at you." When the child does turn to look at the parent during such demanding and forceful commands, the child will typically either have a glazed look over his face, looking completely blanked out, or the child's eyes will be shifting and rolling around. When the parent makes such statements to the child as, "Look at me," the parent is evoking more stress onto an already stressed-out child. The persistent fighting for eye contact only serves to overload the child's dysregulated system with more fear.

A glazed look is a sign of a child dissociating from the parent – and the world. In an effort to endure the overload of internal stress, the child breaks his connection to external stimuli. Internally he is engulfed with stress, thereby having to cut off any additional intake of stimuli in order to merely survive. Hence, the child then presents a frozen look on his face. Similarly, if a child is shifting and rolling his eyes, he is as stressed as the child with the glazed look. It is a sign of a child who has reached his window of tolerance of stress. Traditional attachment therapists have referred to this type of eye movement as "motor eyes"[11] and have interpreted it to be a purposeful behavioral act, targeted directly against the parents. Yet, when the regulatory system is understood, it can be seen that this rolling of the eyes is only a demonstration of the child's dysregulated state.

So, the parent has to move out of the traditional paradigm that says, "Reciprocal eye contact is a pivotal part of making a connection."[12] The parent now has permission with the new view to stop living in fear of not creating attachment because of the lack of eye contact. The enlightened parent can now see this behavior as a communication that the child is simply stressed out – nothing more. With this understanding, parents have permission from neuroscience to help their children, embrace their children, and accept their children in their fear state. Parents can now respond to their children out of love, instead of reacting out of fear.

When Mom sees that Johnny is not making eye contact, she should just stop talking. The talking is adding to the overload of stimulation. It is too much. Mom can then work to calm Johnny through the parent-child relationship, repositioning herself to the side of him, which puts her in a less threatening position, thereby removing the perceived threat. Mom can then divert her gaze to the same direction as Johnny. If he is looking down at the floor, then she can look down at the floor with him – she joins him where he is. By not pressing Johnny to make eye contact, she has just created a more regulated environment. And by joining him in the direction of his gaze, she is meeting her child in his pain, thereby giving him safety to shift back to a place of regulation.

By accepting Johnny's inability to make eye contact, Mom in the above example is preventing the development of a negative neurophysiological feedback loop. Suppose Mom says to her son, "Johnny, I need you to go clean up your room." The negative neurophysiological feedback loop would begin when Johnny puts his head down. If Mom walks over to Johnny and says, "I deserve respectful answers; you need to answer me," the dysregulation in the environment then heightens. From her traditional view, Mom then demands, "Look at me, Johnny." Johnny responds, "I don't want to look at you!" Finally, after more confrontational interactions, Johnny gives Mom a deer-in-headlights gaze. At this point, the environment is full of fear and threat.

Instead, once Mom gives Johnny a directive and receives a shut-down response that lacks eye contact, she then has the opportunity to change the negative neurophysiological feedback loop. Mom can move next to him and if he pulls away, Mom does not even attempt to put her arm around him, but simply accepts that physical touch is adding to his dysregulation. Mom looks down at the floor with him. "Son, what's going on? I can see that you're struggling right now." He moans, "I don't know." Mom responds, "Well, I can tell you're stressed and feeling overwhelmed about something because you can't look at me. You want to talk about it?" "No." Even at this point, the feedback loop has changed because he says "No." instead of "Don't talk to me. I don't want to talk to you!" At that level, Mom can then say, "Son, I'm with you and we're going to be okay," keeping her gaze on the floor. "It is really important that we get this done," still not looking at him. "I need your help; we can work together on this." Mom is communicating with a positive feedback loop. The more positive Mom can be, the less Johnny has a need to escalate in his dysregulation. Remember, the more regulated amygdala has the ability to soothe the more dysregulated amygdala. This fear receptor in our brain communicates via vibrations through the other person. If Mom stays in a positive state, it will encourage Johnny to move to a positive state.

The traditional attachment therapist will say that when a child makes eye contact, it is "on his own terms." When consideration is taken regarding the child's stress state when he is able to make eye contact, it can be easily seen that the child is making eye contact because his neurological system is then in a peaceful, balanced state. He is neurologically able to make eye contact. Thus, these Moments of regulation should be more appropriately celebrated and seen as opportunities to make deep connections with the child. An opening has presented itself for the parent-child relationship to occur. What a shame it would be to miss it!

It is important to recognize that in parenting a child overwhelmed with stress, the parent must allow the process to take its course naturally. Eye contact will happen, but it can only happen when the child is shifted out of his heightened stress state. Lack of eye contact is not "us against them" or "them against us." And is not a "must have" in order for attachment and regulation to occur. Eye contact does not have to be forced, and if it is forced, it is not real.

Therapeutic Example – Lack of Eye Contact

Scenario: Kelly is a seven year old child, adopted from a Russian orphanage at the age of four years old. While in a therapy session one day, her mother was embracing Kelly with soft physical touch. As her mother encouraged Kelly to express and talk about the incident that happened the other day when Kelly turned on all the burners of the stove to "high," Kelly became noticeably anxious and turned her head towards the floor, breaking the eye contact she had previously had with her mother.

Traditional View

The traditional therapist working with this mother and daughter quickly realizes that Kelly needs to be reminded of the first rule of therapy: to have good eye contact while talking together. It is imperative at this point to have Kelly reconnect with her mother in order for Kelly to take ownership of her behavior, and then of her feelings. All discussion of the incident with the stove at this point ceases and Kelly's mother is instructed to insist on eye contact from Kelly. Kelly's mother is instructed to actually *demand* eye contact from Kelly, not to just ask for it. "Look at Mommy! I'm in charge and you need to look at me, Kelly." Kelly resists and the struggle between Kelly and her Mom continues. Kelly refuses to make eye contact. Mom is then instructed by the therapist to show her anger towards Kelly by saying, "Kelly, you make me so mad when you don't look at me. It hurts me and I need you to look at me. Look at me, Kelly!" Kelly turns slightly and begins to look at her mother with a half-focused glance. As this session continues through Kelly's resistance, Mom continues to engage in a vigorous manner, expressing her anger in order to "pop the cork"[15] of all other emotions. Kelly is ultimately able to reach the final stage of resolution with her mother and accept her mother's comfort. With sweat dripping off both Mom and Kelly, Kelly says to her mother, "I was so scared that you were going to send me back to Russia yesterday when the visitors at our house were leaving to go back to Russia." Mom cries with Kelly; they hug and kiss each other.

The session ends after two hours with Mom and Kelly feeling close and content.

New View

The therapist working with this mother and daughter, using the principles outlined in Part I, quickly realizes that Kelly has become overwhelmed with the topic of conversation. Kelly's shift in her eye contact demonstrates an underlying fear of the stove incident. Kelly's mother gently pulls her in closer and says, "Kelly, when you look away from me like that, it only tells me that you're getting too upset about what we are talking about." Kelly's mother reassures her verbally, "Kelly, I love you and nothing you do will ever change my love for you. We're safe and nothing is going to happen to you, sweetheart." Kelly's mother holds her and begins to caress her hair and simply stays present with her, working to calm Kelly's stress response system. After a few minutes, Kelly's mother opens the discussion again by saying, "Kelly, I know it is really hard for you to talk about what you did with the stove, but I'm here with you." As her mother begins to talk about the incident, the therapist encourages the mother to softly request Kelly to make eye contact. The mother, empowered by her own motherly instincts, says to the therapist, "It's okay; she will look at me when she is ready." Kelly's mother expresses her fears over the incident and continues to gently encourage Kelly to talk about her feelings, as well. Spontaneously, Kelly turns to her mother, looks her straight in the eyes, and says, "I was so scared that you were going to send me back to Russia yesterday when the visitors at our house were leaving to go back to Russia." Mom begins to cry and reflect on how scary it must have been to think about being sent back to Russia! Mom relates to Kelly's fears and they hug and embrace each other. Mom reassures Kelly that she will never be sent back to Russia. This 20-minute session ends with Mom and Kelly feeling close, connected, and *safe* together.

Quick Reference **LACK OF EYE CONTACT**

Remember that lack of eye contact:

- Is a signal that the child is in a state of fear and overly stressed.
- Is driven from an unconscious place of fear – it is not a conscious choice by the child.
- Occurs to cut off one of the most direct ways of stimulating the frontal lobe of the brain.
- Happens as a way for the child to keep from over-stimulating his body/mind system.
- Is common in attachment-challenged children because they lack regulatory flexibility.
- Does not determine whether a child can or cannot attach.

When seeing this behavior, recognize that your child needs you to:

- "Listen" to this behavior as it is saying, "I can't take anymore stimulation!"
- Understand that it is an automatic stress response, not a chosen behavior.
- Simply stop talking.
- Reposition yourself into a less threatening position, possibly removing any physical touch for the moment.
- Join him by diverting your gaze to the same place.
- Communicate with a calm and soothing voice.
- Give him emotional and physical space to regulate that is safe, non-confrontational, and accepting.

PART THREE

Parenting Bonus Section

CHAPTER TWELVE

Real-Life Stories from Real-Life Parents with Real-Life Children

∎

Parents who have worked very hard to implement the principles described in this book wrote the following stories. They all volunteered to write their stories in a way to say to you, *"This really does work and my home is now a peaceful place."* These truly are real scenarios with real outcomes, just as the examples given throughout this book were real, as well. The names of the children and many of the locations of the families have been altered in respect of each child's confidentiality and in respect of each child's own personal struggles. So, read on to meet Billy, Chad, Sam, Aaron, Lauren, Jennie, Andrew, Tanika, and another mother who was struggling to implement these principles in the beginning, as well.

Billy (two-and-one-half-years-old)

Billy is our two-and-one-half year old toddler. Through the parenting books that I had read and from the advice of a friend, I had been convinced that Billy needed to be out of his high chair. It was time. I felt it was time for him to be eating and sitting in a regular chair during dinnertime. After all, he would sit in a regular chair at his babysitter's, but not at home with dad and me.

We tried everything from stickers to bribery. But everything we tried ended in tantrums that would often last for hours at a time. Billy would at times become aggressive and physically fight back. Dinnertime became terror time. I remember one night, I tried to bribe Billy into eating in the 'big boy chair.' "Billy, if you sit in the big boy chair and finish your dinner, you'll get to have your favorite dessert. If not, then maybe next time you can have dessert." He became outraged at the thought of not getting dessert. What a disaster it was. *Uggh.* Now I realize that tying a food reward into this very stressful event for Billy was setting the stage for all sorts of eating problems down the road. I now realize that I was not teaching Billy to learn to regulate through relationships, but through rewards and food. Using a reward for the behavior did not address the underlying issue of stress and safety in which Billy was struggling. He really was not able to make a conscious choice of where to sit; he was simply seeking safety that the high chair provided.

Applying the Stress Model, I soon realized that Billy must have felt very safe in his high chair, especially around dinnertime, which is in itself a stressful time in the day for any child (tired, hungry, and maxing out at his threshold of stress tolerance). Dad typically comes home from work, stressed and dysregulated, adding more stress to our home. In addition, I had to reflect on my emotional state. The painful reality was that I was feeling like a failure as a mother because Billy would sit in a regular chair at the babysitter's but not with me, his own mother, at home. What a ton of stress for this child to be contending with!

So, now it's dinnertime and we try a different approach. Tonight, my husband works on creating more regulation within himself and, when he comes home, he works to reconnect with Billy after being gone all day. Dad says, "Hey, Billy, do you want to go play with me before we eat dinner?" Of course Billy jumps at this invitation, and he and Dad spend 20 minutes on the floor playing, talking, and relating. Then, Dad and Billy go set the table together (transitioning into meal time). Dad and Billy get the drinks and set them on the table while I'm finishing up the meal preparation. Dad sits down and has Billy sit on his lap. Then, Dad feeds Billy and nurtures Billy at the table. Then I take a turn, giving Dad a chance to eat, and I feed Billy, as well. I reflect on how Billy's first year of life was spent in a dysregulated environment with little to no food and certainly with no one there to soothe him during what mealtimes were available. After about four nights of doing this, all of a sudden, Billy spontaneously says, "I want to sit in the big boy chair." Magic? No, regulation.

I reflect on what created this change: We all were in tune with one another, regulated, and the environment in the home was peaceful and safe. I realize that Billy was able to make the next step in his own developmental process because we were able to create an environment conducive to growth. It was an environment that provided safety, nurturing, and understanding. I now understand that developmental growth and reaching developmental milestones will happen at Billy's pace, not mine and not a pace determined by anyone but Billy!

— M.H., Charleston, S.C.

Chad (four years old)

I felt defeated, angry and hurt. My husband, my new four year old, and myself were consumed in what I thought was anger. We were told he was a hard case. But I was not ready at all.

Our son was painfully defiant and physically abusive to me and to himself. Yet everyone else with whom we came in contact thought he was an angel.

The nighttime routine really started to take a turn for the worse. I was not calm. I was trying to control him in everything. I was reading different approaches to help with RAD kids. The different approaches would work for a little while, but then things would get crazier. I had to completely take apart his room and monitor his toys. He continued to hurt himself and me. Left alone, Chad would bang his head against the wall and scratch himself. When I tried to keep him from harming himself or things around him, he would get even more violent. It really didn't matter what was going on, Chad came at me in hurtful ways at any given moment. I would firmly say, "You stop that! No!" In trying to hold him, I would be bitten, scratched, and hit.

On one particular evening, I was working out of my home and decided Chad and I would have fun doing some drawing. I tried to stop the drawing to answer the phone. He came at me with a pencil and stabbed my arm. I got the pencil out of his hand and he grabbed my face with his fingernails, screaming, "Do you like that?" I was enraged myself. When we finally got somewhat calmed down he told me, "I am going to cut your head off Mommy. Ha! Ha!" I was completely full of rage. I had no empathy for him, and I left him in his room and told him to stay there, all the while screaming insanely at the top of my lungs – JUSTIFIED.

Then after I calmed down, I realized he was just a baby. I had lost the part of him and myself that was loving. I had forgotten where he came from. And I had somehow forgotten who I was. What was happening here? This is not I! This is not how I want to be!

In the first three months of Chad's placement I tried many things. They all made us psychotic. Our home was a battlefield. We needed a miracle. Then a dear friend introduced me to Bryan Post. I e-mailed Bryan and he got back to me the same day. With a different approach, he got right to the point. His advice was against all I had learned. Instead of trying to control Chad, he told me to just be with Chad and create emotional containment and safety for him. I was just to make sure he wasn't going to hurt himself or others, and I was to stand nearby Chad. Bryan helped me to understand that I needed to be in the same room with Chad in order to help him calm down. I was not to try to approach him. He explained that my son lives in a hyper-aroused state of stress. Chad is full of fear and has been for a long time.

Within the first three days of trying what he suggested, things turned around. It was amazing!

Since that original e-mail, we have been working with Heather Forbes, learning how to implement this parenting paradigm. While this is hard work, my home has been changing in positive ways, everyday. We are healing. I am becoming more self-aware. I now see the fear. And I can more readily get past the angry behavior in Chad. My husband has been in the depths of the healing, also. We are a family.

I wanted something to work a miracle. Looking at Chad as frightened and trying to survive, instead of angry, has been just that miracle. Additionally, this has become a journey for our entire family; it is not just about Chad, it is about our family. It's living at the essence and core of our family. We wanted a more peaceful home. By implementing the Stress Model and the understanding given in this book, we are finding our way.

We thank God for Bryan Post and Heather Forbes. We have been empowered to save our family. And it will help anyone ready to try it with all their hearts.

— T. C., Pinon Hills, Calif.

Sam (six years old)

Going to the grocery store with Sam is never my most enjoyable thing to do. It seems that we can be having a great day until we get to the grocery store. It usually takes about five minutes before all hell breaks loose. I feel my anxiety rising just with the thought of it. Sometimes I break out into a cold sweat, and my stomach churns as butterflies fly around wildly making me want to run. As soon as Sam asks for something and I get ready to give him the dreaded "No," I know it's on the way: his outburst, followed by a resistance to continue down the aisle, and then generally the harsh words, most always spoken very loudly. But, that's not the worst of it. The worst of it are the stares I get from other parents which say, "You're a terrible mom," "Spank that child's little butt," and "If that were my child, he certainly wouldn't be talking to me like that!" It seems as though I'm alone and nobody understands.

After making the paradigm shift and listening to the behavior...

I couldn't believe it would be that simple. Before going to the grocery store, I sat down with Sam and said, "Sam, I love you with all of my heart, but going shopping scares me to death. I feel really scared when we go to the store and I feel like you get really scared also. Today when we go to the store,

I am going to put you inside the basket so I can keep you safe and I'll feel safe as well. It is also important that my love for you is never-ending and just because I will not be buying you anything today does not mean that I don't love you. In fact, the things I will be buying you, you won't even realize are for you, but when we get back home this evening, I will show you. Also Sam, I expect you to ask for things because that is normal for you. Understand that I will say no today, but that does not mean no forever. Do you understand?" We went to the store and Sam asked but did not receive. I felt completely calm in saying no. He even got upset twice and started to yell, but I just stood by him calmly and said, "Hey, I don't blame you for getting mad. I'd get mad also, but remember, today is not forever." Honestly, it was one of the best shopping trips we've ever taken.

— *B.B., Oklahoma City, OK*

Aaron (nine years old)

We had been raising our son, Aaron, using the traditional approach to parenting attachment challenged children for seven long and painful years. One example comes to mind. It seems a little thing, but looking back it was powerful in adding to our son's daily "fear load." I remember our son would always ask us when we were all leaving to go somewhere: "Where are we going?" Aaron would ask the question over and over. We were told to always answer him, "Is that information you need to work on your life?" Likewise, if just my husband and I were leaving and our son would ask where we were going, again, we were supposed to ask him if it was information he needed to work on his life. It seemed harsh, but we figured the professionals knew better than us.

That is WRONG to say to a child. Instead, we should always answer our children to alleviate the fear of the transition and explain to them EXACTLY where we are going, AND the details. They should be reassured that Mommy and Daddy will be right there to keep them safe. Their fear needs to be acknowledged. As in the case when just the parents are leaving, the child should be told, "I know you're scared when Mommy and Daddy leave. I know it is really scary thinking that you won't see us again. I love you and nothing you could ever do would make us leave you."

The traditional theory is "keep the child guessing and feeling out of control because they are NEEDING to control, but making them feel out of control causes them to turn away from their need to control and to trust the parents who are IN control."

My answer: No. It does not. It adds MORE fear. It adds to the child's fear of being scared about whether where the child is going is safe or not; and, likewise, when the parents are leaving, it adds fear for the child about his parents never returning. Remember, two prevalent fears of these children are fear of abandonment and fear of danger. Having been in past environments that were neglectful, abusive or dangerous always has the child in fear of possible danger or of being abandoned.

This traditional model actually fosters the child fearing the very parents he NEEDS to trust in order to heal, because the parents won't tell the child details that would alleviate those fears. How can a child ever trust such a cold, distant parent who leaves him in fear and guessing?

So, I reflect back now and ask myself, "How could Aaron ever have trusted me?" And I painfully answer, "He couldn't have trusted me – what I gave him only furthered his fear, not trust and security."

— *V.W., Altamonte Springs, Fla.*

Lauren (nine years old)

Everyday when I pick-up Lauren from school, I automatically get tense and begin dreading the afternoon; it will soon be homework time! I'd rather have a root canal than do homework with Lauren. She is defiant, resistant, and I feel helpless when trying to help her. When I try to be patient and work through math problems with her or help her answer questions from a story, I feel like I am moving a boulder up a steep incline. So, I tried implementing the Stress Model. "Lauren, today I'm feeling scared that homework time is going to be just like yesterday and just like the weeks past. I'm scared that I'm going to lose my patience and begin yelling. I don't want to yell at you, Lauren. I love you and yelling is not a loving behavior. I want to be able to help you, sweetheart. So, today we are going to take a walk before we begin homework. We're going to talk about your day because I've missed you and I want to know how you're doing. Okay?" Lauren and I have a nice walk; we decompress from the day and discuss where we are emotionally. We go back home and begin homework. I'm thinking, "Okay, I'm doing great. I'm removing the stress; we're going to be able to do this today." After the second math problem, it all begins to break down. I'm staying calm, breathing, and confident that this is going to work. By now, we're on the fourth math problem and she is completely back into the old cycle of resistance and the fear begins mounting. In fact, I'm actually madder today because I expected my efforts to work. Now I'm really mad, thinking, "This Stress Model stuff doesn't work in the real world. It's great in theory, but when the rubber hits the road we're back in the same old place."

Weeks go by of trying to remove the home stress. Continual battles and continual fear fill the air during our afternoons. I go back to using consequences, behavioral rewards, stickers, celebrations, goal setting–whatever I can think of in my time of parental desperation. Nothing works.

Then one afternoon after our daily regiment of defiance, anger, and frustration, I'm with my daughter on the couch just being present with one another. Out of the blue, she pipes up and says, "Mom, I'm scared of going to detention." **THAT'S IT!** I jumped up and said, "Is that what you're scared of when doing your homework, Lauren?" "Yes, Ms. Smith says that if we don't turn in our homework everyday, then on Friday we won't be able to do Fun Friday and we'll have to go to detention. I don't want to go to detention, Mom." As Lauren begins to break into tears, I sit back down with her, and she melts into my arms, sobbing about how scared she is of going to detention. I begin sobbing, "I'm so sorry you've been scared of detention. I'm so sorry. I didn't know."

I called her teacher the next day, explained that Lauren had become so stressed about the threat of going to detention that it was impeding her ability to complete the homework. She agreed to take away this consequence for Lauren with the understanding that if homework did not get done on one day, it would eventually be completed, even if it were over the weekend.

From that moment on, even one year later, Lauren has completed her homework without a single battle. And more importantly, she doesn't face her homework with a threatening black cloud looming over her.

So, yes, the Stress Model really does work. I simply wasn't in tune with the triggering stress for Lauren–it was a threat imposed at school. I was working diligently to remove the stress at home and had overlooked the fact that it was something she was carrying home with her from her school. Lauren is flourishing in school and life after school is fun again.

Next time the rubber hits the road, and it will, I will remember: "Lauren, I can tell that something is upsetting you. What are you afraid of?"

— *J.C., Houston, Texas*

Jennie (10 years old)

As we started out a new school year this August, I was determined to make this year better. I was equipped with the tools I needed and the understanding of the Stress Model. Afternoons were going to be better. Homework wasn't going to be a battle. Pencils weren't going to be broken. There would be no more screaming. We were going to be able to connect when I picked up my daughter. I now understood that she would be dysregulated after being in school all day with 25 other dysregulated children in her fifth grade classroom.

I so wanted it to be different. I was scared, though. The years of picking her up after school were filled with repetitious memories of disconnect, control battles, screaming, tantrums, and worse of all, rageful anger from me of which I was so ashamed. I was scared of it all happening again, but this time I did have a glimpse of hope. I had been an A+ student of the Stress Model and in theory it made so much sense. I knew it explained the dynamics of every fearful situation in my memory of disastrous days and disastrous interactions with my daughter. But could I make the Stress Model happen in reality?

So, I pick my daughter up from her first day of school, her first day in fifth grade. I'm aware of my fear and continue to keep breathing as I open myself up to her in order to reconnect with my little princess. She has difficulty looking me in the eyes, so I breathe. "She's just overwhelmed," I tell myself. "Eye contact is just too intense for her sensory system." I breathe. I begin to engage verbally with her. I say, "Well, how was your first day of school, Jennie?" She says, "Fine." I breathe. There's no initiation to give details, no attempt at meeting me in relationship. I expand on my question, "On a scale of one to ten, with ten being the best and one being the worst, how would you rate your day?" My "sweet little princess" replies, "It was a B."

Judas! I can't do this. My body tightens up. Every effort to relate to her has just been met with resistance. She only gives me pieces and then she gives me pieces that don't even connect with what I'm saying–"B! What happened to the scale of one to ten?" I breathe. Her response feels passive aggressive, distant, and aloof. I breathe. I then relate how my sister, who looked just like my daughter at her age, was passive-aggressive towards me growing up. I breathe. I realize my reaction is about feeling like I'm talking to my sister. I silently speak to myself, "She's not my sister...she's my daughter." I breathe.

By now I'm shifting back into a state of love and my rational brain is getting some oxygen. I realize that my daughter just had her first day of school after being home with me for the past three months of summer vacation–an entire summer at home where she felt safe and secure. I realize that she is in a state of stress. I realize that my daughter has been around stressful people for the past six hours, including the principal and the teachers (they're always nervous the first day of school, fearfully working to make everything run smoothly). I realize that she was actually trying to make connection with me, but that stress causes her brain to be full of "cobwebs" and she really can't think straight right now. In fact, she gave me an answer that really did address my question, and I realize that she was quite creative in setting the scale to the same scale as the environment she was in the whole day.

So, I put my arm around her and said, "I missed you today, princess. I'm glad you had a good day."

After being in school for three weeks, it is different and we now have fun after school. I realize that when I receive responses like the above example that she isn't being intentionally controlling, manipulative, or passive aggressive. She truly is not using these responses to keep me at a distance. In fact, it is quite the opposite. When I receive these types of responses, it is a communication that she needs me more than ever to help her shift from a place of dysregulation to a place of regulation through my relationship with her. What a different year we are going to have!

— *S.F., Lansing, Mich.*

Andrew (12 years old)

I really don't know where to begin about how this New View has helped our family. From the first one-day presentation by Bryan Post here in Las Vegas, I knew I had found a way of looking at parenting my three adopted children that would actually work. At the time I went to the seminar, we were tied up with multiple workers in the house trying to bring some order to the chaos of our lives. They all kept trying to have us implement reward charts and behavior modification techniques that were actually increasing my stress while being incredibly ineffective with our children. I felt so vindicated when Bryan Post stated that for some children these methods do not work and actually create worse behaviors. I immediately began implementing the few techniques I knew while making plans to attend the next intensive training. My husband will tell you I came back from the seminar and said, "WE ARE GOING!"

When we are aware of our own dysregulation and hot buttons, we are much better able to focus on helping our children. I find that when we are in public, I am always stressed as to how my children ages eight, 10 and 12 are going to behave. A problem that we were having with our 12 year old was that he would not use a public restroom. Andrew has limited control of himself due to early trauma in his life and remains disconnected from his bodily signals, so many times he doesn't know he has to use the restroom until the need is unbearable. At those times he would run around holding himself, which is rather embarrassing behavior in a large boy who looks 14 to 15 years old. I found myself in just such a situation at the ballpark one day. I took three deep breaths and calmed him down enough to talk to him about why the problem kept occurring. Andrew told me that he was afraid he would make a mess of the bathroom and have to clean it up. This fear went back to an embarrassing and traumatic incident he had over a year before at school. When I was able to approach the problem in a calm regulated manner, I was able to help him regulate through his fears. We no longer have this type of problem. Though this may seem like a minor problem, it is the minor dysregulated events that occur each day, every day, over and over during the day, that add up to overwhelm and meltdowns. So being able to help Andrew in these small ways are really monumental experiences of healing.

— *A.B., Las Vegas, Nev.*

Tanika (14 years old)

Our daughter, a budding teenager, suffered extreme neglect in foster care as a young child. At the ages of 11 and 12, she was hoarding food in her bedroom. During a "cleaning sweep" one day, my wife found numerous bags of snacks, uneaten sandwiches, fruit and candy in the drawers of Tanika's desk in her bedroom. These were mixed with empty bags, empty soda cans, and other food trash.

We cleaned everything out, but left all the foodstuff in the middle of her room so we could talk about it with her. We learned from the seminars that her hoarding was probably a sign of deep fear and insecurity. We learned that she was satisfying a deep need through stealing, hiding, and eating food in secret.

When Tanika came home from school, we walked with her to her room. As we entered, she was immediately embarrassed and apprehensive. But we gently told her that we were sorry that we had not realized how afraid she was and that we now understood that she was using food to fight the fear. We told her that we left the food there as a reminder to us of how we had failed her, how we had failed to be able to meet her needs. We told her that if she was ever tempted to take food and hide it, we wanted her to come to us. We explained that what her body was telling her was that she needed physical refueling and we could give that to her through our affection and hugs. We encouraged her to see that what she really needed was a hug from her Mom or Dad. Whether it was day or night, anytime she felt afraid and would have gotten food, we encouraged Tanika to come to us and say simply, "Mom/Dad, I need a hug."

This approach has given Tanika freedom to speak to us about her fear and also provides us, as her parents, a better way to meet our daughter's fears and insecurities. And Tanika gets what she really needs–affection– rather than food. Once she gets the affection, the gnawing need and urges for food disappear.

— *M.B., Orlando, Fla.*

Mother (45 years old)

My family did an in-home intensive following this model. During those three days, I heard the message...ANGER IS FEAR...over and over again. I heard it, I bought it, and yet I could not use it in any effective way with my own daughter.

I heard the message about how it could be possible that parents dealing with their child's attachment issues can also revisit their own trauma history during their early years. That also made sense, but did not seem to apply to me, or my early life. I had always believed I was raised in a fairly normal environment—no incest, no abuse and no early traumatic event that seemed especially harrowing to me. My parents did not believe in corporal punishment, and I was spanked only one time that I could remember. So obviously, this very reasonable theory did not apply to me.

Bryan Post told me during our sessions that I was afraid of my daughter and her anger. I assured him he was wrong—dead wrong. But actually, he was right on with his analysis of my behaviors. I was too ashamed of my childish responses to my daughter's rages to allow him to see how very terrified I was of her anger. I did not want him to see how I would freeze, become numb and actually dissociate during her rages. I did not want him to see how completely ineffective I was in handling my own daughter's fear responses.

Unfortunately, I was unable to utilize any of the techniques learned during the intensive as I was in worse shape than my daughter. I was ashamed of my lack of response to her behaviors and usually would either begin to hysterically laugh or stand frozen in time and space. Obviously, I was unable to calm her as I could not calm myself. And more importantly, I could not understand my responses or my own terror. It did not make sense. And since it did not make sense, I could not move past the seemingly insurmountable obstacle of soothing and calming myself, let alone my terrified child.

One day, several years after the intensive, I was driving my car, and for some reason I began to think about my sister. And I began to remember her rages during my early years....rages that went on for hours and were the focal point of our family life for years. This was something I always knew, and years after it was remembered as one of the family jokes, but I never questioned how it affected MY life. For the first time I asked myself this question, "I wonder how it felt to me as an infant and toddler to experience one of my sister's wild and earsplitting rages?"

Bingo, there was my answer and there also was my surprise. The trauma experience does not have to be obvious and it does not have to be something most people would consider to be shattering or life changing. But traumatic it was and it affected my responses to anger and fear for my entire life.

It was gratifying for me to see that as soon as I could identify the reason for my fear, I was able to believe in it and could begin to deal with it. I was finally able to begin to soothe my daughter when she would rage because

I could identify my own childish reactions to her anger and see it for what it was....a childish and long- ago fear of something that I had no control over at the time. But as an adult, I was no longer in danger from my sister's early behaviors.

— N.A., Los Angeles, Calif.

Questions and Answers

▪

The following Q&A section comes from the Beyond Consequences eNewsletter. This eNewsletter is a free service of BCI. We invite you to log into our homepage to sign-up now so you don't miss another issue:

www.beyondconsequences.com

QUESTION:
How can I help prepare my child for social situations like a trip to the dentist or getting a haircut? He becomes so defiant and then, when I finally do get him there, it typically turns into a disaster. So, my next question is, how can I then handle the situation effectively when it does not go so well?

ANSWER:
In order for parents to prepare their children for social situations like going to the dentist or getting a haircut, it is important for parents to realize that the underlying issue behind the resistance is fear. When parents can address the children's fear and calm their children's stress, these situations do not have to be such hurdles anymore. Simply seeing a child as a scared child, as opposed to a resistant child, allows the parent to provide safety and reassurance at an entirely new level.

Parents can help to calm their children before they even leave the home. Sitting with the child, physically touching the child through an embrace or a touch on the arm or shoulder, the parent can then talk with the child. Being attuned from the child's emotional perspective, not an adult perspective, is a key task. We tend to rationalize, minimize, and normalize our children's fear saying, "Oh, it won't be so bad. Don't worry." Instead, if the child's fears are truly heard and the parent can validate the child's fears, without feeling like they have to convince the child to feel differently, the child will then have the emotional space to find his own courage and feel secure enough in the parent/child relationship to move forward.

If the parent has done everything to help the child at an emotional level and the child still continues to be unable to move through these situations in an appropriate way, then it is not a reflection of the parent. Too many times parents take this personally; they are embarrassed by their children's behavior, and they invalidate themselves as parents based on the children's inability to respond to the parent's efforts. The reality is that it is not about the parent. It is simply about the child not being ready. Ironically, the more the parent can give the child the emotional space and accept the child's lack of readiness, the more the child will then be able to work through these situations in the future.

Adding more stress to the child through many well-intended parenting strategies such as incentives and rewards can actually be detrimental. An already stressed out child may not be able to handle the stress of receiving or not receiving a reward. We need to respect our children's natural path of development. Respecting our children in the present, while realizing that they will find their way with parental acceptance, love, and support around them, is a valuable lesson for them to learn.When we work to connect and support our children, they learn that they are perfectly acceptable and unconditionally loved. This is what provides the safety for them to then take the next steps in their development—not external rewards or incentives. I promise you they won't be 18 years old and still scared to get a haircut! And more importantly, they won't have bad memories of relational disconnect with their parents around such events.

QUESTION:
I have a 12 year-old daughter who was adopted at birth. As it turns out, she has multiple problems including Tourrette's syndrome, severe ADHD, OCD, and possible ODD. She has always had trouble sleeping and until last summer would get up at night and either go through the kitchen looking for sweets or get into trouble in a variety of ways. After listening to your CDs, I realized that this was caused by fear. I started lying down with her at night for a couple of hours and then moving to my own bed. But now she is waking up later and wanting to get in bed with me. Now my sleep is interrupted several times a night and has been for almost six months. I thought she would eventually adjust, but things seem to be worse than ever in terms of her being able to sleep on her own. Also, I have been struggling with breast cancer for about a year now and really need my sleep. I would let my husband help, but she does not want him. How do I ease her into a more independent sleeping pattern?

ANSWER:
You have done an excellent job of identifying that your daughter's sleep difficulties are related to fear. Many children who wake up in the middle of the night are in a state of dysregulation, hence in a state of fear. They get up, seeking something to soothe them. Just like you or I; what do we eat when we are stressed out? Chocolate? Candy? Something sweet!

There is a part of the brain called the Nucleus Accumbens that programs this quest for sweets. This is the part of the brain where you feel pleasure.

There are three tastes that this part of the brain craves: salt, sweets, and fats. Thus, she was seeking sweets to feel better and relieve the discomfort that comes with being emotionally dysregulated. By lying down with her, you were helping to interrupt this need to regulate through sweets. She was regulating herself through her relationship with you. Congratulations! Now to address the next issue: that she continues to wake up throughout the night and she has not adjusted.

Since your daughter has not been able to sleep straight through the night, it is an indication that the core issue has not been addressed. It isn't that you've created a child who now wants to wake you up in the middle of the night; this shift is simply a part of the process. I would celebrate that she is waking you up instead of going to the sugar in the cabinet. After acknowledging this achievement, we then need to look at the next level to ensure that both of you are getting the proper sleep. So what is the core issue that has not been addressed?

I believe the core issue is something you mentioned briefly at the very end of your note and that was, "I have been struggling with breast cancer for about a year now." Take a deep breath and take the time to understand the impact that this statement has on this situation. Since she doesn't want dad during these times of stress, she is communicating that her fear is with you.

It has been my experience that every child who was adopted, whether at birth or later in life, has abandonment issues. Your struggle with breast cancer can only be a trigger to her fear of loss and abandonment. Even if she wasn't adopted, the potential for her to be struggling with the threat of losing you would be tremendous. So, I am not "blaming" the adoption experience, simply identifying the intensity of the core issue of abandonment.

It is imperative that you be truthful to yourself about your own fears. Breast cancer is scary. You are being challenged at a deep emotional and survival level yourself. Opening yourself up to your fear of dying and the other fears that come along with this disease is going to be pivotal in helping your daughter. As you are in touch with your fear, you will then be able to open yourself up to your daughter's fear.

Perhaps her fear is shutting you down and then she is feeling emotionally abandoned and waking up in the middle of the night, which is then stressing you out and then adding more stress to her and... So the cycle of fear is then being fed between the two of you and neither of you is getting enough sleep.

I encourage you to talk with your daughter. Share your fears that have been ignited with the struggle of breast cancer. Create the emotional space for her to tell you what is stirring up inside of her. She may have the words. She may not. Yet, in either case, as you share your core fears, she'll have the permission to identify her fears and then share them with you.

The important piece of sharing is to remember that you are not responsible for fixing this situation for her. You simply make the commitment to her that your family will bind together through this difficult time and you make the commitment to everything you can to find healing. Encourage her to share her emotions with you so that she does not have to keep them all locked up during the day, only to be faced with the fullness of the emotions in the middle of the night.

Stay focused on the core issue instead of the outcome of a more independent sleeping pattern. Sometimes it takes encouraging more dependent behaviors (like connecting at an emotional level) in order to develop independent behaviors!

QUESTION:
My son, now six years old, is very controlling in his behaviors. Although he was not adopted and did not go through many of the experiences of the children of your readers, his birth experience was difficult. When my wife was eight months pregnant, I received a call from her doctor that she had an aneurism and that he was concerned that she might die and/or that the baby might die. The next month was an incredibly stressful time for our family and my son was born a few weeks later by C-section. I was told that mom and baby were just fine. Could my son be attachment-challenged even though he has been with us since birth and could this birth experience have anything to do with his behaviors now?

ANSWER:
Birth trauma has an incredible impact on our development. I don't believe we truly understand the depth of such experiences and the influence they may have on our physical, emotional, spiritual, and cognitive development for our entire lives. Your son came into this world in terror ... read that again: terror! He entered life overwhelmed by the fear of death. His mother was fearful not only for her own life, but also for his life. All those feelings were transferred to his little system. It is important to realize that he did not have the internal resources to handle such an experience and thus, those feelings were stored in the cells of his body, his unconscious memory, and now his system is programmed for survival. His controlling behaviors are a direct reflection of this.

In order to help children process through these early life experiences, they need to hear their stories. They need to be able to make sense of what happened and they need to be able to start the process of connecting the emotions with words and cognitive thought. Begin this process by sitting by your wife and having your son lying on your laps, holding him close. Talk to him about what happened when he was in "mommy's tummy." And more importantly, express yourselves to him from a deep emotional level. Words alone will not connect with this time in his life. Trauma happens on an emotional level, especially preverbal trauma such as this. Cry for him, cry together as a couple, cry for yourselves.

Let him know that you now realize how scared he was. Let him know that you understand now that he was absolutely terrified. Don't be afraid to use the words, "Son, you thought you were going to die." These are not new ideas you are planting in his head. These feelings are already inside of him and he is acting out of them on a daily basis. You'll be giving him the words to finally make the connection and thus, helping him to lay the path for healing. Also, take ownership of this experience for him by apologizing to him. Children are egocentric and automatically react within by thinking it is their fault. I would guess that your wife feels a level of guilt and this will help her to process through her feelings, opening up the gateway for a deeper level of attachment, ultimately helping your son to strengthen his bond with you both. As this connection is strengthened, his need to control will dissipate as he develops a sense of safety and security.

QUESTION:
I understand that my adopted daughter has a trauma history but if I'm not giving consequences, then doesn't my child think that her behavior is okay? I'm struggling because it isn't acceptable to be disrespectful to me. I have to say that her behavior is appalling! I understand how reacting can be disempowering—but what can I do that's empowering in that moment that sends the right message to her?

ANSWER:
If we go back to the understanding that negative behavior comes from an unconscious place (see Chapter 1), we can begin to see that the disrespect is about something much deeper. This level of disrespect began in early relationships where her own needs were never respected. She is simply acting out of the model that was imprinted within her system in years prior. As our book mentions, those are the patterns that bind us. If you work to change the behavior in the moment of her distress, you will find yourself becoming frustrated at the lack of change. This is because we cannot learn when we are stressed out. Stress inhibits our cognitive thinking. So the life lesson of being respectful even when angry needs to come when she is calm and regulated. Work to calm her nervous system and calm her emotional state. Really listen to her. Many times children (and we, as adults) become disrespectful, rude, and/or loud because we don't feel like we are being heard. Connect with the disrespect instead of trying to shut it down.

When you truly listen to what is behind the disrespect, you will find the depth of pain and fear your daughter is experiencing. Saying something like, "Sweetheart, when you speak disrespectfully, that only tells me that you're hurting inside. It also tells me that someone must have really disrespected you." (Feel that pain for her, apologize for how she was treated, join her instead of correcting her, etc.) She needs you to help her to connect with her pain; it is too painful and too scary to connect with it on her own. She is reacting at you because feeling her level of pain is overwhelming to her entire system. Thus, the message you will be sending back to her at that very moment is one of respect, compassion, and love. You will be giving her the message that strengthening your relationship with her is your primary goal-that she is more important to you than anything else on this planet.

Certainly the long-term goal is to teach our children to be respectful to their parents and that we should all be respectful. Yet when this lesson is given in the heat of the moment, defensive, disrespectful, and defiant feedback loops are created between parent and child (see Chapter 4). And the most important point is:

> *The real consequence is that relationships become broken and the relationship's focus becomes control and power.*

So, an hour later, that evening, or sometime when you both are better connected, talk to her about the disrespect and discuss options and ways to handle it differently the next time. Express your reactions to her behavior and how it makes you feel. Perhaps relate a story of your own experience from your past that would connect with her. All of this will begin to help her to learn how to connect with herself when she begins to get stressed out and dysregulated. This will empower her to come to you for help in a loving and respectful way and it will empower her to develop her own regulatory ability to handle stressful situations as an adult.

Parenting out of this love-based approach is hard work. In most cases, it would be much easier to give out a consequence and be done with it. Yet, when we truly understand that behavior does not come from a cognitive, rational place, we realize that giving consequences is actually quite irrational and illogical. The Beyond Consequences Institute (BCI) was not established to help parents and professionals simply learn a new technique. Rather, BCI is about learning an entirely new paradigm. It is a paradigm that you live out of and a paradigm in which your perspective of the world is forever changed— a perspective whose foundation is based in love and in the understanding that power does not come from control, but through loving influence.

QUESTION:
I was just wondering what you would suggest we do about a foster child who

pulls hair and hits the other children in the home.

ANSWER:
Pulling hair and hitting are signs of a child who is threatened by other children. This can be especially true for foster children who have come from stressful environments. Many children with such trauma histories are literally living in survival mode. Their internal voice is saying, "If I dominate over you, I will be first in line to have my needs met." It is a sign of a child who is simply acting out of a primal place to ensure his/her survival.

As you work to go beyond the behaviors and understand how threatened this child is feeling, you'll understand that giving this child consequences for acting out is likely to intensify the acting out. Consequences will create more insecurity, thus the child will feel more threatened, more stressed, and more overwhelmed. For this child, fighting with another child in the home, especially a younger child, may be the only "logical" way to create more security for himself.

Going back to the understanding that all behavior arises from a state of stress, you would then want to begin calming the stress for this child. When the child pulls the hair of another child or hits another child, check in briefly with the child who was hurt, acknowledging his pain and then saying, "I'm going to go take care of 'Johnny' because he is feeling really scared right now. I want to make sure everyone is safe, so I'll be right back."

When you approach Johnny, I'm certain his early blueprints will be expecting you to be angry and at some level he will be expecting to be punished. Instead, breathe deeply to calm your own nervous system, put your arm around him if he will let you, and say, "Johnny, you're safe with me. How about you and I have some special time together and read a book on the couch right now?" This is called "Time-In," and it is a way to pull the child out of the stressful interaction and reconnect in relationship with him.

I realize that we may not always be able to stop everything and sit down and read a book. It can be something as simple as coming into the kitchen with you while you finish cooking dinner or being with you while you are folding the laundry (he might even help out once he calms down). The goal is to just be together so you can create security for the child through your relationship. In this time together, avoid mentioning the behavior at first. Talk about the rest of his day, get to know him more by asking about his interests, favorite foods, favorite super hero, etc.

As he relaxes, you can then help him understand that when he becomes overwhelmed and scared, he might feel like he needs to hurt one of his foster siblings. Give him permission to come get you. Put yourself out there to be the safe base that he needs. Assure him he will not get in trouble by coming to you for help. Commit to helping him feel safe within his own home by check-ing in with him more while he is interacting with his siblings.

As you take responsibility for your part in the home, you are teaching him to take responsibility for his actions. Many times, you'll see a child initiate an apology once his stress state is calm and he is regulated because you have done the same for him.

And you're asking, "But what about the sibling who was hurt? Isn't this teaching the agressor to get attention by acting out?" If we truly understand that children act out because they NEED attention, not just because they want it, our stress over this question will subside. We certainly need to recon-nect with the injured sibling and apologize for not making the home a safer place for him.

We may want to then have some Time-In with this child in order to provide him with more security and love so he does not feel compelled to be revengeful against Johnny.

Children develop their perception of siblings through their parents. If the parent perceives Johnny as the "bad" child or the "aggressive" child, the siblings will reinforce this perception in their interactions with this child. This only promotes more of the same, and in this example, would keep Johnny at arms length to any type of meaningful relationship in the home ... with anyone.

Young children need parental interaction while playing with one another. Parents serve as regulatory figures within this social context. In other words, the parents help to keep the playtime regulated, calm, and safe. Older chil-dren who have not had positive social experiences will also need a parent or adult to help do the same.

You wouldn't leave a couple of two year olds in a room for an extended period of time; so likewise, you wouldn't leave two ten year olds with the emotional/social maturity of two year olds in a room for an extended period of time. It may take more "checking-in" during this playtime to ensure safety and to decrease the social stress. Eventually, they will learn, but it is our re-sponsibility as parents to provide the environment for learning.

Through your relationship with your child, however long that may be for a foster child (one month, six months, three years...), you have the "power" to build that child's regulatory system and help your child develop a greater window of stress tolerance so he/she can better handle life's stressful situa-tions. Children (and adults) heal through relationships. Keep working to see beyond the painful, aggressive, and spiteful behaviors in order to capture the moments of great healing!

QUESTION:
My family (and I mean the whole family) is looking for interventions for issues that have gotten bigger than us. We have had a lot of success, but we need to keep moving forward. I don't know where to go from here ... we are open to anything. My husband and I are worn down and finding it harder and harder to get in the place we need to be in to help our children. It has been over three years since they came into our home. One is six and the other is seven—full siblings. Help!

ANSWER:
The daily "grind" of it all can be wearing and difficult. I really hear you. Parenting children with trauma histories is so much more than having a particular technique or using a specific method. In order to sustain yourself and your family, it will take an entirely new reality.

This new reality requires that you commit to taking responsibility for your family, which is evident in your question. You've got this critical piece, so now how to get there ....

Your new reality will only work when you are not a victim anymore. While you may not do this consciously, when you get tired, it is easy to slip into making yourself a victim of your situation. When you get caught up in feelings of overwhelm, helplessness, and frustration, these feelings create a reality that does not work because they shift you to a place of victimhood. In order to move out of this reality and to move into a new reality, you have to take control at all times.

Oh no ... there's that word: control! But control means self-control: staying focused in your life and being mindful. It means keeping yourself regulated and attuned to the environment around you. I define control here as staying in a place of love, commitment, and acceptance of who you are and who your child is.

While I will suggest some resources to support you, the most important concept to accept is that nobody is going to make it work for you except for you. Love is your responsibility. Personal peace and acceptance from within cannot come from an outside source. It is about you becoming your own best friend. This then equips you to keep unveiling the mask of anger, façade of disrespect, and coating of manipulation your children present to you daily. What your children present to you is really an illusion. Behind the anger, behind the disrespect, and behind the manipulation is a scared child, desperately in need of connection, love, and acceptance.

If you are your own best friend, you are then in a place where you are unshakable. No matter what behaviors they present, you are able to lift the behavioral veil, to see their truth of internal fear, and in many cases, terror.

As you learn to ground yourself in the truth of their behaviors (and yours), you will be able to permanently change your frame of reference. Staying mindful and focused keeps you from falling back into the old familiar frame of reference that says they need a good spanking or that they need to have consequences.

The reality is that the emotional pain of "finding it harder and harder" is actually your gauge, or indicator, that you are shifting back to victimhood. Pain is only an indication of something not working. Pain is also an indication of resistance. Embrace your pain because it is getting you to rise above your old frame of reference.

It takes intention and commitment to regain yourself, or what is referred to as taking back your "personal power," to release yourself from the victimhood. Again, nobody can make it work for you except for you.

Along with this internal development and work needed, I would also like to identify some adjunctive resources that are designed to support you:

1. There is an online support group with parents and professionals from around the world that are working to implement the Beyond Consequences model. It can be found at:
   http://heatherforbes.ning.com

2. BCI has several free audio recordings to deepen your understanding of the principles discussed in this book. Simply log on to the following website:
   www.beyondconsequences.com/freeaudios.html

3. My favorite suggestion for parents needing a resource to stay focused and regulated is called "Dare to Love Yourself." This CD set has been shown to help parents stay in a place of love during behavioral outbursts. It's like having a coach at your fingertips 24 hours a day. Available at:
   www.beyondconsequences.com/store.html

4. I have several trainings scheduled and I would love to have you join me for a great day of training. You can sign-up at:
   www.beyondconsequenceslive.com.
   The full-day training is FREE simply with a copy of any of my books.

5. One more option is "Phone Coaching." Phone coaching allows you to work individually with a Beyond Consequences trained therapist. Many families have used this service as a way to check in for support and to further develop understanding for their specific situations. Feel free to call the BCI office for more information if you are interested at (407) 965-1131.

You are the instrument of peace, so keep pressing on!

For more Q&A responses from Heather T. Forbes, LCSW, sign up for our eNewsletter! It's FREE and it will keep you empowered and energized. Log onto:
www.beyondconsequences.com

Epilogue

■

W hen an epilogue is included in a novel or short story, it is typically used to tell what eventually happened to the main characters. Or, as Paul Harvey might say, to give "the rest of the story." Well, the main characters in this book are our children. So what happens to all the children of the world who have suffered trauma and are demonstrating their pain and emotional states of fear through severe behaviors?

The answer to this question absolutely scares me. I experience a trembling in my heart when I reflect on the perception of our children that is being offered by professionals in the field of attachment. A chilling example of why I fear the *rest of the story* for our children is in the following graphics:

A   B   C

Sources:
A. Thomas, N.L. (1997). *When love is not enough: A guide to parenting children with RAD-reactive attach- ment disorder.* Glenwood Springs, CO: Nancy Thomas.
B. Magid, K., & McKelvey C. A. (1987). *High risk children without a conscience.* New York, NY: Bantam Books.
C. Randolph, E. (1997). *Children who shock and sur prise: A guide to attachment disor- ders.* Evergreen, CO: PDQ Printing

These pictures come directly off the covers of books written with the intent of offering understanding of our children's behaviors with attachment issues. Take a few moments to really study these three teddy bears. Feel your reaction to these images at a body level. For me, my stomach becomes queasy, my arms tingle, and my forehead tightens and scrunches up in disgust.

What kind of understanding do these images offer? They do not offer hope and they certainly do not offer truth. They simply stir-up fear. They feed more fear into parents who are already at their brink – at a point where they already feel like the darkness has closed in on them.

I understand the logic behind these images. It is an attempt to show the dichotomy of love and terror, where the teddy bear represents what children should be cuddly, lovable, and tender, while contrasting this to the literal mutilation of the teddy bear, a representation of the terrorizing behaviors many attachment-challenged children exhibit. And yes, many of our children have done much worse than cutting off an arm of a stuffed animal and have gone beyond an inanimate object to do horrible acts to living animals.

Yet, reinforcing this through the depiction of images, titles, and captions only creates more division between the child and the parent. Thus, the true dichotomy here is the resultant contrary effect these images have on the goal of *building* bonds and *strengthening* attachments! One cannot build and strengthen a relationship when fear is present. (*There is no fear in love–* 1 John 4:18).

Recently, an article was published in a popular family magazine, *Family Circle* (October 18, 2005). The article's title alone, "The Boy Who Could Not Love," sets the stage for believing that love is beyond the main character's (the adopted child) capacity. The article goes on to depict a child with severe acting out behaviors who at three years old, is labeled as a danger to those around him. The article, with one caption reading, "The Mad Monster," perpetuates the traditional view that these children are angry and "flatly refuse" to be loved.

In order for our children to heal, we need to go beyond what is seen and we must go *beyond consequences, logic, and control* in our interactions with our children. The love-based understanding explained in this book delineates between the conscious and the unconscious. Thus, it is not about a child who consciously "refuses" to be loved, rather it is about a child who is engulfed in fear from an unconscious body level. Candace Pert, in her audio CD, *Your Body Is Your Subconscious Mind*, tells us that we are biologically designed to be in bliss. At a biological, primal level, we are designed to be happy! Our children need us to trust that they truly are capable of returning to this state of bliss, given an environment of love that fosters this return to happiness.

And, of course, we are designed for happiness, for we are made in the image of God (*For in the image of God has God made man.–*Genesis 9:6)! This truth also exists outside the realm of religion. Bruce Lipton, an internationally recognized cell biologist, came to this exact conclusion through his scientific studies and research. In his book, *The Biology of Belief*, he explains that even the smallest of proteins within our bodies require a connection with our environment and that these proteins are completely dependent on environmental signals to function. Thus, he concludes, "we are made in the image of the environment, that environment being the Universe, or to many, God."

When we stray away from this truth and remain constricted in fear, seeing our children in the image of anger, manipulation, or defiance, we limit everything about our children. We limit their biological programming. We limit our relationships with them. We limit their healing potential. We limit their futures. And turning full circle, we limit God.

So to write this epilogue, depicting what eventually happened to the main characters, I want to write:

"Parents, teachers, and caregivers shifted their paradigms and began to see our children from a love-based perspective. It was finally seen that consequences, logic, and control destructively interfered with our children's God-given ability to heal and to return to a state of bliss. No child was ever again deemed beyond help and no child was ever again deemed 'unadoptable.' Relationships strengthened and families soon lived in peaceful and loving homes."

This is no fairy-tale and all of the above truly is possible! May you continue on your healing journeys and may you continue to have the tenacity, commitment, and empowerment to shift from a place of fear to a place of love.

Press on!

–Heather Forbes, ~~LCSW~~ "MOM"

Recommended Readings
■

Resources for Parents:

Brazelton, T.B. (1992). *Touchpoints: Your child's emotional and behavioral development*. Reading, MA: Addison-Wesley Publishing.

Brazelton, T.B. & Greenspan, S. (2000). *The irreducible needs of children: What every child must have to grow, learn, and flourish*. Cambridge, MA: Perseus Publishing.

Breggin, P. (2000). *Reclaiming our children: A healing solution for a nation in crisis*. Cambridge, MA: Perseus Books.

Chopra, D. (1994). *Journey into healing*. New York: Harmony Books.

Clark, N. & Post, B. (2005). *The forever child: A tale of loss and impossible dreams*. Mountain View, OK: M. Brynn Publishing.

Clark, N. & Post, B. (2003). *The forever child: A tale of fear and anger*. Mountain View, OK: M. Brynn Publishing.

Clark, N. & Post, B. (2002). *The forever child: A tale of lies and love*. Mountain View, OK: M. Brynn Publishing.

Covey, S.R. (2007). *The 8th habit: From effectiveness to greatness*. New York, NY: Free Press.

Davis, P. (1999). *The power of touch: The basis for survival, health, intimacy, and emotional well-being*. Carlsbad, CA: Hay House.

Eldridge, S. (1999). *Twenty things adopted kids wish their adoptive parents knew*. New York, NY: Dell Publishing.

Forbes, H.T. & Post, B.B. (2006). *Beyond consequences, logic, and control: A love-based approach to helping attachment-challenged children with severe behaviors,* Volume I. Orlando, FL: BCI.

Forbes, H.T. & Dziegielewski, S. (2003). *Issues facing adoptive mothers of children with special needs*. Journal of Social Work 3 (3). (Available for download at: www. beyondconsequences.com)

Goldman. D. (2006). *Social Intelligence*. New York, NY: Bantam Books.

Goleman, D. (1994). *Emotional intelligence: Why it can matter more than IQ*. New York, NY: Bantam Books.

Granju, K. & Kennedy, B. (1999). *Attachment parenting: Instinctive care for your baby and young child.* New York, NY: Pocket Books.

Hanh, T. (1987). *Being peace.* Berkeley, CA: Parallax Press.

Harris, B. (2008). *Confident parents, remarkable kids: 8 principles for raising kids you'll love to live with.* Avon, MA: Adams Media.

Harris, B. (2003). *When your kids push your buttons and what you can do about it.* New York, NY: Warner Books.

Hanessian, L. (2004). *Let the baby drive: Navigating the road of new motherhood.* New York, NY: St. Martin's Press.

Hart, A. (1992). *Stress and your child.* Dallas, TX: Word Publishing.

Jamplosky, G. (1979). *Love is letting go of fear.* Berkley, CA: Celestial Arts.

Karen, R. (1994). *Becoming attached: Unfolding the mystery of the infant-mother bond and its impact on later life.* New York, NY: Warner Books, Inc.

Karr-Morse, R., & Wiley, M.S. (1997). *Ghosts from the nursery: Tracing the roots of violence.* New York: Atlantic Monthly Press.

Kohn, A. (2006). *The homework myth: Why our kids get too much of a bad thing.* Cambridge, MA: Da Capo Press.

Kohn, A. (2005). *Unconditional parenting: Moving from rewards and punishment to love and reason.* New York, NY: Atria Books.

Liedloff, J. (1986). *The continuum concept.* New York, NY: Penguin Books.

Perry, B. & Szalavitz M. (2007). *The boy who was raised as a dog: And other stories from a child psychiatrist's notebook – What traumatized children can teach us about loss, love, and healing.* New York, NY: Basic Books.

Rosenberg, M. (2003). *Nonviolent communication: A language of life.* Encinitas, CA: Puddle Dancer Press.

Sears, W. & Sears, M. (2001). *The attachment parenting book: A commonsense guide to understanding and nurturing your baby.* New York, NY: Little, Brown and Company.

Selye, H. (1974). *Stress without distress.* New York, NY: Signet.

Siegel, D. & Hartzell, M. (2003). *Parenting from the inside-out: How a deeper self-understanding can help you raise children who thrive.* New York, NY: Jeremy P. Tarcher/ Putnam.

Tolle, E. (1999). *The power of now.* Novato, CA: New World Library.

Verrier, N.N. (1993). *The primal wound: Understanding the adopted child.* Baltimore, MD: Gateway Press.

Additional Resources for Professionals:

Bowlby, J. (1988). *A secure base: Parent-child attachment and healthy human development*. New York, NY: Basic Books.

Bowlby, J. (1980). *Attachment and loss: Vol. 3 Loss: Sadness and depression*. New York: Basic Books.

Bowlby, J. (1973). *Attachment and loss: Vol. 2 Separation and anger*. New York, NY: Basic Books.

Bowlby, J. (1969). *Attachment and loss: Vol.1 Attachment*. New York, NY: Basic Books.

Bremner, J. (2002). *Does stress damage the brain?: Understanding trauma-related disorders from a mind-body perspective*. New York, NY: W.W. Norton and Company.

Carnegie Corporation (1994). *Starting point: Meeting the needs of our youngest children: The report of the Carnegie task force on meeting the needs of young children*. New York, NY: Carnegie Corporation of New York.

DeGangi, Georgia. (2000). *Pediatric disorders of regulation in affect and behavior*. New York, NY: Academic Press.

Frattaroli, E. (2001). *Healing the soul in the age of the brain*. New York, NY: Penguin Books.

Greenspan, S., and Cunningham, A. (1993, August 22). *Where do violent kids come from?* Charlotte Observer, reprinted in the Washington Post.

Janus, L. (1997). *Echoes from the womb*. Livingston, NY: Jason Aronson.

Justice, B., & Justice, R. (1990). *The abusing family*. New York, NY: Plenum Press.

Kandel, E.R. (1998). *A new intellectual framework for psychiatry*. American Journal of Psychiatry, 155, 457-469.

LeDoux, J. (1996). *The emotional brain: The mysterious underpinnings of emotional life*. New York, NY: Touchstone.

Levine, P.A. (1999). *Healing trauma: Restoring the wisdom of the body*. (Audio Cassette Recording). Louisville, CO: Sounds True, Inc.

Levine, P.A. (1997). *Waking the tiger, healing trauma*. Berkley, CA: North Atlantic Books.

Lipton, B. (2005). *The biology of belief: Unleashing the power of consciousness, matter, and miracles*. Santa Rosa, CA: Mountain of Love/Elite Books.

McEwen, B.S. (1992). Paradoxical effects of adrenal steroids on the brain: Protection vs. degeneration. *Biological Psychiatry 31*, 177-199.

McEwen, B. (1999). Development of the cerebral cortex XIII: Stress and brain development – II. *Journal of the American Academy of Child and Adolescent Psychiatry, 38*, 101-103.

Montagu, A. (1986). *Touching: The human significance of the skin.* New York, NY: Harper and Row.

National Center for Clinical Infant Programs (2005). *Diagnostic classification of mental health and developmental disorders of infancy and early childhood.* Arlington, VA: Zero to Three.

Perry, B.D. (2002). Childhood experience and the expression of genetic potential: What childhood neglect tells us about nature and nurture. *Brain and Mind, 3*, 79-100.

Perry, B.D. & Pollard, R. (1998). Homeostasis, stress, trauma and adaptation: A neurodevelopmental view of childhood trauma. *Child and Adolescent Psychiatric Clinics of North America, 7*(1) 33-51.

Perry, B.D. (1997). Incubated in terror: Neurodevelopmental factors in the "cycle of violence." In J. Osofsky (Ed.), *Children in a violent society* (pp. 124-149). New York, NY: Guilford Press.

Perry, B.D. (1996). *Maltreated children: Experience, brain development, and the next generation.* New York, NY: W. W. Norton.

Perry, B.D. (1996). *Neurodevelopmental adaptations to violence: How children survive the intergenerational vortex of violence, Violence and childhood trauma: Understanding and responding to the effects of violence on young children,* Gund Foundation, Cleveland.

Perry, B.D., Pollard, R.A., Blakely, T.L. Baker, W.L., & Vigilante, D. (1995). Childhood trauma, the neurobiology of adaptation, and "use-dependent" development of the brain: How states become traits. *Infant Mental Health Journal, 16*, 271-291.

Perry, B.D. (1993). Neurodevelopment and the neurophysiology of trauma: Conceptual considerations for clinical work with maltreated children. *The Advisor, American Professional Society on the Abuse of Children, 6*:1.

Pert, C.B. (2004). *Your body is your subconscious mind* (Audio CD Recording). Louisville, CO: Soundstrue, Inc.

Pert, C.B. (2004). *Psychosomatic wellness: Healing your bodymind* (Audio CD Recording). Magic Bullets, Inc.

Pert, C.B. (1997). *Molecules of emotion.* New York, NY: Touchstone.

Ross, C.A. (2000). *The trauma model*. Richardson, TX: Manitou Communications.

Sapolsky, R.M. (1990). Stress in the wild. *Scientific American 262*, 116-23.

Scaer, R.C. (2005). *The trauma spectrum: Hidden wounds and human resiliency.* New York, NY: W.W. Norton & Company, Inc.

Schore, A.N. (1994). *Affect regulation and the origin of the self.* Hillsdale, NJ: Lawrence Erlbaum Associates, Publishers.

Schore, A.N. (2003). *Affect regulation and the repair of the self.* New York, NY: W.W. Norton.

Shapiro, F. & Forrest, M. (1998). *EMDR: The breakthrough therapy for overcoming anxiety, stress, and trauma.* New York, NY: Basic Books.

Siegel, D.J. (1995a). Memory, trauma, and psychotherapy: A cognitive science view. *Journal of Psychotherapy Practice and Research, 4,* 93-122.

Solomon, M.F. & Siegel, D.J. (Eds.). (2003). *Healing trauma: Attachment, mind, body, and brain.* New York, NY: W.W. Norton & Company.

About the Authors
■

Heather T. Forbes, LCSW

Heather T. Forbes, LCSW, is the owner of the Beyond Consequences Institute. She is an internationally published author on the topics of adoptive motherhood, raising children with difficult and severe behaviors, and self-development. Forbes lectures, consults, and coaches parents throughout the U.S., Canada, and Europe, with families in crisis working to create peaceful, loving families. She is passionate about supporting families by bridging the gap between academic research and "when the rubber hits the road" parenting. Much of her experience and insight on understanding trauma, disruptive behaviors, developmental delays, and adoption-related issues comes from her direct mothering experience of her two internationally adopted children.

B. Bryan Post

B. Bryan Post is the founder of the Post Institute for Family-Centered Therapy. He is an internationally recognized specialist in the treatment of emotional and behavioral disturbance in children and families. Post specializes in a holistic family-based treatment approach that addresses the underlying interactive dynamics of the entire family, a neurophysiologic process he refers to as, "The secret life of the family." As an adopted, and well-known disruptive child himself, ("I've set fires, killed animals, and stolen compulsively.") Post has made it his primary work to speak to parents and professionals from a perspective of true-life experience and in the 'trenches' of therapeutic work.

.

Endnotes

.

Chapter 1

1 LeDoux, J. (1996). The emotional brain: The mysterious underpinnings of emotional life. New York, NY: Touchstone.

2 Perry, B. (2003). Keynote address. Eye Movement Desensitization and Reprocessing
International Association Conference. San Diego, CA.

3 Candace Pert (2000). Your body is your subconscious mind. [CD] Louisville, CO: Sounds True, Inc.

Chapter 2

1 Randolph, E.(1997). Children who shock and surprise: A guide to attachment disorders. Evergreen, CO: PDQ Printing.

2 Levy, T. M., & Orlans, M. (1998). Attachment, trauma, and healing: Understanding and treating attachment disorder in children and families. Washington, D.C.: Child Welfare League of America, Inc.

3 Pert, C.B. (1997). Molecules of emotion. New York, NY: Touchstone.

4 Perry, B. D. (2002). Keynote and Breakout Sessions:. EMDR International Association 2002 Conference. San Diego, CA.

5 Covey, S. (2006). The 8th Habit: From Effectiveness to Greatness. New York, NY: Simon & Schuster.

6 LeDoux, Joseph (1998). The emotional brain. New York: NY: Touchstone.

7 Schore, A.N. (1996). The experience-dependent maturation of a regulatory system in the orbital prefrontal cortex and the origin of developmental psychopathology. Development and Psychopathology, 8:59-87.

8 Bowlby, J. (1988) A secure base: Parent-child attachment and healthy human development. New York, NY: Basic Books.

9 Schore, A. N. (1994). Affect regulation and the origin of the self. Hillsdale, NJ: Lawrence Erlbaum Associates, Publishers.

10 Schore, A.N. (2003). Affect dysregulation and disorders of the self. New York, NY: W.W. Norton & Company, Inc.

11 Sroufe, L. A. (1995). Emotional development. New York, NY: Cambridge Univer-

sity Press.

12 Pert, C.B. (1997). Molecules of emotion. New York, NY: Touchstone.

13 Perry, B. D. (2003). Keynote Session. Neurons to Neighborhood 2003 Conference. Los Angeles, CA.

Chapter 4
1 Schore, A.N. (2003). Affect dysregulation and disorders of the self. New York, NY: W.W. Norton & Company, Inc.

2 Goldman, D. (2002). Emotional intelligence. New York, NY: Bantam Books.

Chapter 5
1 Thomas, N.L. (1997). When love is not enough: A guide to parenting children with RADreactive attachment disorder. Glenwood Springs, CO: Nancy Thomas.

2 Delaney, R. J. (1998). Fostering changes: Treating attachment-disordered foster children. Oklahoma City, OK: Wood 'N' Barnes Publishing.

3 Cline, F. W., & Helding, C. (1999). Can this child be saved? Franksville, WI: World Enterprises.

4 Keck, G. C. & Kupecky, R. M. (1995). Adopting the hurt child: Hope for families with special-needs kid. Colorado Springs, CO: Pinon Press.

5 Thomas, N.L. (1997). When love is not enough: A guide to parenting children with RADreactive attachment disorder. Glenwood Springs, CO: Nancy Thomas.

6 Hughes, D. (1998). Building the bonds of attachment: Awakening love in deeply troubled children. Northvale, NJ: Jason Aronson, Inc.

7 Keck, G. C. & Kupecky, R. M. (1995). Adopting the hurt child: Hope for families with special-needs kid. Colorado Springs, CO: Pinon Press.

8 Ward, S. (2002). Adoptive parenting – maintaining control. Retrieved May 15, 2005, from http://www.suite101.com/article/cfm/adoptive_parenting/95611

9 Cline, F. W., & Helding, C. (1999). Can this child be saved? Franksville, WI: World Enterprises.

10 Keck, G. C. & Kupecky, R. M. (1995). Adopting the hurt child: Hope for families with special-needs kids. Colorado Springs, CO: Pinon Press.

11 Forbes, H. & Dziegielewski, S. (2003). Issues facing adoptive mothers of children with special needs. Journal of Social Work 3 (3).

12 Covey, S. (1989). The 7 habits of highly effective people: Restoring the character ethic. New York, NY: Simon & Shuster, Inc.

13 Fearon, R. M. P., & Mansell, W. (2001). Cognitive perspectives on unresolved loss: insights from the study of PTSD [Electronic version]. Bulletin of the Menninger

Clinic, 65 (2).

14 Davis, J. L., Petretic-Jackson, P. A., & Ting, L. (2001). Intimacy dysfunction and trauma symptomatology: Long-term correlates of different types of child abuse [Electronic version]. Journal of Traumatic Stress, 14 (1).

15 Horowitz, M. J., M.D. (1997). Stress Response Syndromes. Northvale, NJ: Jason Arson, Inc., p. 146.

16 Munson, C. E. (1995). Overview of diagnosis and treatment of psychological trauma in children. Early Child Development and Care, 106, p. 163.

17 Copping, V. E., Warling, D. L., Benner, D. G., & Woodside, D. W., (2002). A child trauma treatment pilot study. Journal of Child and Family Studies, 10 (4), p. 468.

18 Hughes, D. (1998). Building the bonds of attachment: awakening love in deeply troubled children. Northvale, NJ: Jason Aronson, Inc.

19 Pert, C. (1997). Molecules of emotion. New York, NY: Touchstone.

20 Keck, G. C. & Kupecky, R. M. (1995). Adopting the hurt child: Hope for families with special-needs kids. Colorado Springs, CO: Pinon Press.

21 Thomas, N.L. (1997). When love is not enough: A guide to parenting children with RADreactive attachment disorder. Glenwood Springs, CO: Nancy Thomas.

22 Cline, F. W., & Helding, C. (1999). Can this child be saved? Franksville, WI: World Enterprises.

Chapter 6

1 Levy, T. M., & Orlans, M. (1998). Attachment, trauma, and healing: Understanding and treating attachment disorder in children and families. Washington, D.C.: Child Welfare League of America, Inc.

2 Magid, K., & McKelvey C. A. (1987). High risk children without a conscience. New York, NY: Bantam Books.

3 Delaney, R. J. & Kunstal, F. R. (1997). Troubled transplants: Unconventional strategies for helping disturbed foster and adopted children. Oklahoma City, OK: Wood 'N' Barnes Publishing.

4 Cline, F. W., & Helding, C. (1999). Can this child be saved? Franksville, WI: World Enterprises.

5 Hage, D. (n.d.) Antecedents to lying and teaching the truth. Retrieved June 4, 2005, from http://www.fosterparents.com/articles/Dhage.html

6 Ibid.

7 Ward, S. (2002, January 5). Adoptive parenting – tips for parenting the tough ones. Retrieved May 14, 2005, from http://www.suite101.com/article.cfm/adoptive_parenting/88312

Chapter 7

1 Cline, F. W., & Helding, C. (1999). Can this child be saved? Franksville, WI: World Enterprises.

2 Levy, T. M., & Orlans, M. (1998). Attachment, trauma, and healing: Understanding and treating attachment disorder in children and families. Washington, D.C.: Child Welfare League of America, Inc.

3 Cline, F. W., & Helding, C. (1999). Can this child be saved? Franksville, WI: World Enterprises.

4 Thomas, N.L. (1997). When love is not enough: A guide to parenting children with RADreactive attachment disorder. Glenwood Springs, CO: Nancy Thomas.

5 Keck, G. C. & Kupecky, R. M. (1995). Adopting the hurt child: Hope for families with special-needs kid. Colorado Springs, CO: Pinon Press

6 Magid, K., & McKelvey C. A. (1987). High risk children without a conscience. New York, NY: Bantam Books.

7 Portsmouth Herald (March 28, 2004). Last of the small-time bank robbers. Retrieved June 5, 2005 from http://www.seacoastonline.com/2004news/03282004/accent/7743.htm

8 Center for Family Development (n.d.). An overview of reactive attachment disorders for teachers. Retrieved April 30, 2005, from http://www.center4familydevelop.com/helpteachrad.htm

9 Smith, L. B. (n.d.) Oil and water: The attachment disordered child in school. Retrieved June 5, 2005, from http://www.attachmentdisorder.net/helpforteachers.htm

Chapter 8

1 Keck, G. C. & Kupecky, R. M. (1995). Adopting the hurt child: Hope for families with special-needs kid. Colorado Springs, CO: Pinon Press.

2 Delaney, R. J. & Kunstal, F. R. (1997). Troubled transplants: Unconventional strategies for helping disturbed foster and adopted children. Oklahoma City, OK: Wood 'N' Barnes Publishing.

3 Thomas, N.L. (1997). When love is not enough: A guide to parenting children with RADreactive attachment disorder. Glenwood Springs, CO: Nancy Thomas.

4 Keck, G. C. & Kupecky, R. M. (1995). Adopting the hurt child: Hope for families with special-needs kid. Colorado Springs, CO: Pinon Press.

5 Levy, T.M. & Orlans, M. (1998). Attachment, trauma, and healing. Washington, D.C.: CWLA Press.

6 Magid, K., & McKelvey C. A. (1987). High risk children without a conscience. New York, NY: Bantam Books.

7 Thomas, N.L. (1997). When love is not enough: A guide to parenting children with RADreactive attachment disorder. Glenwood Springs, CO: Nancy Thomas.

8 Personal communication from a father of a child diagnosed with reactive attachment disorder, describing the explanation of a previous attachment therapist. (2004).

9 Thomas, N.L. (1997). When love is not enough: A guide to parenting children with RADreactive attachment disorder. Glenwood Springs, CO: Nancy Thomas.

10 Hage, D. (n.d.). Children behave the way they behave. Retrieved May 13, 2005, from http://www.deborahhage.com/articles/childrenbehave.htm

Chapter 9

1 Hage, D. (n.d.). "Going to your room" practice. Retrieved May 13, 2005, from http:// www.deborahhage.com oom.htm.

2 Keck, G. C. & Kupecky, R. M. (1995). Adopting the hurt child: Hope for families with special-needs kid. Colorado Springs, CO: Pinon Press.

3 Hopkins-Best, M. (1997). Toddler adoption: The weaver's craft. Indianapolis, IN: Perspectives Press.

4 Keck, G. C. & Kupecky, R. M. (1995). Adopting the hurt child: Hope for families with special-needs kid. Colorado Springs, CO: Pinon Press.

5 Ibid.

6 Cline, F. (1979). Understanding and treating difficult children and their parents. Golden, CO: Love and Logic Press.

7 Hughes, D. (1998). Building the bonds of attachment: Awakening love in deeply troubled children. Northvale, NJ: Jason Aronson, Inc.

8 Hage., D. (n.d.). Paradoxical techniques: Resisting resistance increases resistance. Retrieved April 30, 2005, from http://www.deborahhage.com/articles/childrenbe-haveparadoxicaltechniques2.htm

9 Federici, R. S. (1998). Help for the hopeless child: A guide for families. Alexandria, VA: Hennage Creative Printers.

10 Hage, D. (n.d.). Paradoxical techniques: resisting resistance increases resistance. Retrieved April 30, 2005, from http://www.deborahhage.com/articles/ childrenbehaveparadoxicaltechniques2.htm

11 Cline, F. W., & Helding, C. (1999). Can this child be saved? Franksville, WI: World Enterprises.

Chapter 10

1 Hughes, D. A. (1997). Facilitating developmental attachment: The road to

emotional recovery and behavioral changes in foster and adopted children. North-vale, NJ: Jason Aronson, Inc.

2 Thomas, N.L. (1997). When love is not enough: A guide to parenting children with RADreactive attachment disorder. Glenwood Springs, CO: Nancy Thomas.

3 Federici, R. S. (1998). Help for the hopeless child: A guide for families. Alexandria, VA: Hennage Creative Printers.

4 Hage, D. (n.d.). "Going to your room" practice. Retrieved May 13, 2005, from http://www.deborahhage.com oom.htm

5 Hughes, D. A. (1997). Facilitating developmental attachment: The road to emotional recovery and behavioral change in foster and adopted children. Northvale, NJ: Jason Aronson, Inc.

6 Levy, T.M. & Orlans, M. (1998). Attachment, trauma, and healing. Washington, D.C.: CWLA Press.

7 Delaney, R. J. (1998). Fostering changes: Treating attachment-disordered foster children. Oklahoma City, OK: Wood 'N' Barnes Publishing, p.89.

8 Goble, W. Lecture at the ATTACh conference (1999) – example given in lecture.

9 Levy, T.M. & Orlans, M. (1998). Attachment, trauma, and healing. Washington, D.C.: CWLA Press, p. 205.

10 Cline, F. & Fay, J. (1990). Parenting with love and logic: teaching children responsibility. Colorado Springs, CO: Pinon Press.

11 Thomas, N.L. (1997). When love is not enough: A guide to parenting children with RADreactive attachment disorder. Glenwood Springs, CO: Nancy Thomas.

12 Ibid.

13 Ibid.

14 Goldman, D. (2002). Emotional intelligence. New York, NY: Bantam Books.

15 Ward, S. (2002). Adoptive parenting – tips for parenting the tough ones. Retrieved May 14, 2005, from http://www.suite101.com/article.cfm/adoptive_parenting/88312

16 Hage, D. (n.d.). "Going to your room" practice. Retrieved May 13, 2005, from http://www.deborahhage.com oom.htm

Chapter 11
1 Levy, T.M. & Orlans, M. (1998). Attachment, trauma, and healing. Washington, D.C.: CWLA Press.
2 Ibid.

3 Hughes, D. A. (1997). Facilitating developmental attachment: The road to emotional recovery and behavioral change in foster and adopted children. Northvale, NJ: Jason Aronson, Inc.

4 Magid, K., & McKelvey C. A. (1987). High risk children without a conscience. New York, NY: Bantam Books.

5 Levy, T.M. & Orlans, M. (1998). Attachment, trauma, and healing. Washington, D.C.: CWLA Press.

6 Keck, G. C. & Kupecky, R. M. (1995). Adopting the hurt child: Hope for families with special-needs kid. Colorado Springs, CO: Pinon Press.

7 Ibid

8 Hughes, D. A. (1997). Facilitating developmental attachment: The road to emotional recovery and behavioral change in foster and adopted children. Northvale, NJ: Jason Aronson, Inc.

9 Welch, M. G. (1990). Holding time. New York: NY: Fireside.

10 Thomas, N.L. (1997). When love is not enough: A guide to parenting children with RADreactive attachment disorder. Glenwood Springs, CO: Nancy Thomas.
11 Magid, K., & McKelvey C. A. (1987). High risk children without a conscience. New York, NY: Bantam Books.

12 Hage, D. (n.d.). Foundations of attachment. Retrieved July 13, 2005, from http://www.deborahhage.com/foundations.htm.

13 Thomas, N.L. (1997). When love is not enough: A guide to parenting children with RADreactive attachment disorder. Glenwood Springs, CO: Nancy Thomas

14 Ibid.

15 Welch, M. G. (1999) Video Series: Welch Method Attachment Therapy: Creating & Repairing Attachment with Direct Synchronous Bonding.

Index
■

abuse 5, 7, 11, 12, 33, 34, 39, 85, 115
adoption 5, 85, 119
aggression 18, 27. 71-79, 83, 89
amygdala 14-16, 19, 26, 48, 63, 73, 76. 79, 95
anger 8, 11-13, 29, 33-43, 66, 71, 72, 75, 77, 78, 82, 84, 91, 96, 105, 108-110, 115, 125, 131
anti-social 46, 81
attachment-challenged 46-47, 53, 61-62, 81, 94, 98, 118, 130
attachment disorder 11, 21, 91
attachment therapy 11, 24, 91

bedtime 13, 84-86, 89
blaming 38, 40, 51, 56, 119
brain 6, 9, 12, 14-16, 18, 37, 47-48, 55, 59, 63, 72, 79, 87, 92, 95, 98, 110, 119
bipolar 5
body-mind 13, 15, 37, 48, 84,93
bottle-feeding 65
Bowlby, John 17

cells 7, 18, 37, 74, 118
chores 13-14, 82, 86,
circadian rhythms 63
communication 23-24, 26, 55-56, 76, 86, 89, 91-92, 94, 111
consequences 47, 56, 85, 109, 119, 123
containment 56, 59, 78, 105
Covey, Stephen 14, 35

defiance 8, 12, 19, 81-89, 109, 131
depression 13, 55, 86
dinnertime 64, 72, 103-104
disobedience 4, 9, 11, 24, 81
disrespect 25, 57, 66, 76, 84, 88, 121-122, 125
dysregulation 17, 54, 75, 77, 95, 111, 118

eye contact 26, 83-93, 104

feedback loops 4, 23-29
fight 8, 15, 25, 39, 46, 73, 83, 94, 123
fire-setting 8
flight 6, 15, 83
food 50, 61-69, 104, 112, 121
foster care 74, 77, 84, 112, 123
freeze 6, 15, 83, 89, 113

Goleman, Daniel 26, 86
gorging 27, 61-69

healing 38, 40, 43, 46, 49, 86, 106, 112, 120, 124, 131

Order Form

■

Books	Quantity	Cost	Total

Beyond Consequences, Logic, and Control:
A Love-Based Approach to Helping
Children with Severe Behaviors

    1 to 4 copies: $19.95 each
    5 to 10 copies: $17.95 each
    11 to 25 copies: $15.95 each
    26 to 50 copies: $13.95 each
    (Prices good for both Volumes 1 and 2)

Dare to Love
    (Prices same as above)

100 Daily Parenting Reflections
A Love-Based Parenting Nuggets to
Encourage You Daily
    $9.95 each

DVD

Beyond Consequences Live!
4-set DVD
If you've been unable to attend a Beyond Consequences Live training event, here is your solution. Intensive role plays on this dynamic DVD will give you "real-life" examples to equip you as a parent with "real-life" solutions.
    $109.00 each

Audio CD's

Beyond Consequences for
Toddlers, 5 to 9's, Tweens, Teenagers
9-disc Audio CD Set
This 9-part audio CD set will bring you solutions and to a deeper understanding of the books *Beyond Consequences, Logic, and Control*. These discussions hit the mark for children of all ages and put the concepts of this book into action.

Price: $97.00

Shipping Costs _____

Total Cost _____

Payable to:

Beyond Consequences Institute
1630A 30th Street, #488
Boulder, CO 80301
www.beyondconsequences.com

Shipping and Handling Scale:
up to $25.00 .... $ 5.95
$25.01 - $45.00 .... $ 7.95
$45.01 - $90.00 .... $ 9.95
$90.01 - 140.00 .... $ 12.95
$140.01 - 190.00 .... $ 14.95
$190.01 - 240.00 .... $ 16.95
$240.01 - 290.00 .... $ 18.95
over $290.01 .... please call